The Pruning Handbook

£12.99

The PRUNING Handbook

Steve Bradley

The Crowood Press

First published in 1996 by
The Crowood Press Ltd
Ramsbury, Marlborough
Wiltshire SN8 2HR

**British Library Cataloguing in Publication
Data**

A catalogue record for this book is available
from the British Library.

ISBN 1 85223 981 6

Photographs by Valerie Bradley.

Line illustrations by Claire Upsdale.

Typeface used: Plantin.

Typeset and designed by
D & N Publishing, Ramsbury,
Marlborough, Wiltshire.

Printed and bound by
Paramount Printing Limited, Hong Kong.

Contents

Introduction

Perhaps the most mystifying element of gardening is the question of when, how (or indeed why) to prune plants. What is pruning? Put in its simplest form, it is a means of controlling plant growth, productivity and shape by cutting and training.

To the fruit grower, for whom this ancient art is standard practice, this form of plant manipulation is essential, as it ensures reliable cropping. In the case of ornamental plants, rose pruning and hedge trimming are the practices most frequently carried out and documented. However, for most trees and shrubs, pruning is performed as a remedial operation rather than a routine one. It is common for an ornamental plant to be pruned only when it begins to encroach on a neighbour or over a path.

Pruning can be the answer to making an unproductive tree fruitful, but do not expect miracles! Years of neglect cannot be rectified in one season. The unknowing pruner who cuts because he thinks he ought to (without knowing how or why) can finish up with a plant which bears no flowers or fruit at all as a result of over-severe pruning or because the pruning operations have been carried out at the wrong time of year.

Aesthetic pruning, for those gardeners who are obsessed by tidiness and formality, and where trees and shrubs conform like soldiers on a parade ground, is done for entirely different reasons. Trees are ruthlessly lopped to a standard height and shape, shrubs cut back to a predetermined size and shape with all being as close to identical as is possible. The difficulty with this being that no heed is paid to the different growth rates of the plants.

Striving for precise, uniform growth is really only necessary in a *parterre*, which is laid out in a symmetrical geometric design where lines have to be kept sharp, or with the practise of topiary, where a sculptured appearance is desired.

An evergreen plant regularly pruned into a predetermined formal shape.

The power of pruning; this conifer has been carefully trained into a spiral shape over the years (left).

An urban plane tree, pruned to reduce shade and prevent individual branches becoming too large.

REASONS FOR PRUNING

Pruning can be described as the removal of a part or parts of a woody plant by man for a specific purpose. The reasons for pruning are:

1. to train the plant
2. to maintain plant health
3. to obtain a balance between growth and flowering
4. to improve the quality of flowers, fruit, foliage or stems
5. to restrict growth

Training

A woody plant will come into flower earlier if it is allowed to grow naturally. Pruning delays flowering, but in the early years it ensures a framework of strong, well-spaced branches, later to produce flowers and fruit. A tree of the desired size and shape can be fashioned which is not only well-balanced and delightful to the eye but carries flowers or fruits where they can be easily seen and reached. Building up an initial framework means easier management of the tree, shrub or climber in later years.

A stub of dead growth left on the trunk of a tree. This is a site through which pests and diseases can easily enter, and invade healthy tissue.

Maintaining Health

A healthy tree is a beautiful one! Control of pests and diseases is essential and it is easiest if the cause of these afflictions can be removed as early as possible. Pruning is one way in which this can be done. In the early stages, pests and diseases interfere with training; in an aged specimen, they hasten the end; whilst at all stages of growth, they are unsightly, can destroy flowers or fruit and weaken branches. The fall of a large branch can mean severe damage or even death to the tree.

Routine spraying can control pests and some diseases in shrubs and young trees but it becomes impracticable (if not impossible) on large trees, when pruning is the only feasible method of control. Most of the diseases which attack trees enter through wounds and then spread via the vascular tissue which conducts water, minerals and starches throughout the plant.

Once infection occurs, branches are killed as they succumb to the spread of the disease and if the trunk becomes infected, the plant will die. The disease organism travels beyond the wood it has killed and, before very long, apparently healthy sections of the plant become infected. This can usually be detected by a brown interior staining. When diseased wood is being removed, *always* cut back to sound wood (wood where there is no staining). Dead wood is always unsightly and likely to break off, causing damage. It is the main source of disease which can spread from the dead wood to the live (e.g. coral spot), so always remove it.

Optimizing Growth and Flowers

A tree or shrub in strong, active growth produces few flowers and over-heavy pruning can delay or even prevent flowering. Pruning in the early years should be sufficient only for training. Once a tree has come into full flowering, shoot production will decline until, at maturity, very little annual growth is being added.

In a mature plant, it is the young wood which produces leaves and, in many plants, even the flowers, whilst with age the quality of these and the rate at which they are produced declines. It is therefore desirable to encourage a woody plant to maintain the production of some young wood by judicious pruning.

Improving Flowers and Fruit

The more flowers and fruit a plant produces, the smaller they become, as can be witnessed on an unpruned rose bush or fruit tree. Pruning reduces the amount of wood and so diverts energy into the production of larger, though fewer, flowers and/or fruit. The length of flower spikes on an unpruned *Buddleja davidii* (butterfly bush) may be 10cm (4in) but can exceed 30cm (1ft) on one that has been pruned hard.

Leaves are produced only on current season's growth. The more vigorous this is, the larger will be the leaves, and in plants with coloured leaves, the more intense will be the colouring. Some deciduous shrubs have coloured barks which are especially colourful in winter. The best colour is produced on young stems and the greatest length and most intense colour results from hard pruning.

Restriction of Growth

Trees and shrubs that are left to develop naturally grow bigger and bigger, becoming a problem where space is restricted and so pruning becomes necessary to keep them within bounds.

OTHER FORMS OF PRUNING

There are some jobs carried out in a garden which are also forms of pruning although they are not always recognized as such. The cutting of flowers from woody plants for home decoration is a type of pruning. The

A selection of the knives and secateurs which are often used for pruning plants.

trimming of hedges is restrictive pruning applied to a row of shrubs. Topiary, which is the clipping of bushes into bizarre shapes, is a combination of training and restrictive pruning, and so is pleaching, used to make living screens or arches. Tree surgery is an extreme form of pruning to maintain a mature tree in a healthy condition.

SELECTING THE RIGHT EQUIPMENT

Secateurs, long-handled pruners (loppers), saws, knives, and long-arm pruners all have their place when pruning, with shears being more useful for shaping and trimming. Always remember that the right tool for the job makes the task in hand much easier.

Secateurs

The best tool for most types of pruning is a pair of sharp secateurs. There are four main types available, with a wide range of variations on these basic types being sold.

The first is the anvil type, which has a single straight-edged cutting blade closing down onto an anvil, a bar of softer metal (often brass).

The second is the parrot bill type, which has two curved blades bypassing one another very closely and cutting in a scissor-like fashion.

The third type has two blades both with straight cutting edges which meet as the cutting action is completed. These are called Manaresi type.

The fourth, and most commonly seen, is the blade and half-anvil type, which has one convex-shaped cutting blade. This cuts past a second curved bar which is fixed, and works by a bypass cutting action.

A useful modification to some of the models which have an anvil cutting action is the ratchet type, which enables the user to cut through a branch in stages. These are

very good for reducing fatigue. They are ideal for gardeners with a smaller hand span, but the cutting action is slower than that of conventional models.

Each of these types can produce good clean cuts if they are used correctly and provided they are kept clean, sharp and in good condition.

Always position the stem to be cut close to the base of the blade where it can be held firmly. If the cut is made with the tip, the blades are liable to be strained or forced apart.

Long-Handled Pruners

These are basically strong secateurs with long handles which give extra leverage when cutting fairly thick stems or branches. They are extremely useful for dealing with old stems on such vigorous shrubs as *philadelphus* and for cutting out the old stumps which gradually build up at the base of bush roses. They are also known as 'loppers'.

Long-Arm Pruners

These are used for pruning tree branches which would normally be out of reach, and are capable of cutting through branches up to 3cm (1¼in) thick. They consist of a pole 2–3m (or yards) in length, with a hooked anvil and curved blade at the tip. The blade is operated by a lever at the opposite end. There are models available with a small basket attached close to the blade, these are recommended by some manufacturers for picking fruit without the need to use a ladder. However, great care has to be taken not to remove next year's fruit buds when using this device at harvest time.

Pruning Saws

These will be required for cutting larger branches. Several designs are available which are especially suitable for use in small spaces and in the narrow angles between branches.

The English pruning saw has a tapering blade with teeth on both sides, one set producing a smoother finished cut than the other. Care has to be taken not to damage nearby branches with the set of teeth not in use and for this reason, some gardeners prefer a tapered version of the normal carpenter's saw.

The Grecian saw, which has a curved blade tapered to a sharp point and sloping teeth designed to cut on the return stroke, is also very useful in confined spaces. Many of these saws are designed to fold, with the blade closing into the handle (like a knife), and fit neatly into a pocket when not in use. They are really only capable of cutting through smaller branches.

Hand Shears

These are available in several designs. Regardless of which particular model is chosen, they should be well-balanced, strong, light and comfortable to use, with a sharp cutting edge. Most have straight blades with a deep notch at the base of the blade for cutting thicker stems. There are models available with a wavy-edged blade which prevents the plant growth being squeezed back out of the mouth of the shears.

It is important to use good quality, well-made tools and to keep them in good condition, so that they will last for a long time. This means making sure they are kept sharp, and cleaning and oiling them after use to prevent them from rusting. Never be tempted to cut through wood which is too thick for the tools you are using; you will only strain the tools, make the cutting action less effective, and put severe strain on your wrists and arms when applying excessive pressure. This is because the natural tendency is to wrench and twist while cutting through a branch which is too thick. This causes strain and often results in a jagged cut, which in turn is much more prone to invasion from pests and diseases.

Pruning Knives

These can be easily identified by their weight, the bulky appearance of the handle and concave blade. The curve of the blade helps when cutting through thicker branches.

A selection of the saws, shears, loppers and long-arm pruners in common use today.

CHAPTER 1

Basic Techniques

When plants are pruned or trained, the main objective is to obtain the best possible ornamental display or maximum crop from any selected specimen. However, it may also be important to retain a particular shape or appearance whilst at the same time striking a balance between healthy vigorous growth and encouraging the production of flowers and fruit.

Many trees and shrubs do not need rigorous annual pruning to fulfil these aims and after their initial training may need no more than minor 'cosmetic pruning'; that is a gentle control of nature involving the removal of spent flowers and cutting out of thin, weak or crossing shoots to maintain an overall balanced shape. On the other hand, formally clipped hedges or topiary work involve not only firm, early training, but careful and timely pruning if they are to be kept in a well-tailored condition.

Pruning will stimulate a plant into producing more stems, so cutting the top growth of a large over-vigorous plant may result in creating more not less growth. Here, pruning may still be the answer, but a change of method may be the key. Directing attention away from the top of the plant down towards the base of the main stem for bark ringing, or even to the roots for root pruning, can often bring better results.

BASIC PRINCIPLES OF PRUNING

Before beginning to prune any plant, it is essential to have a basic understanding of it's growth and flowering habit, and in particular the time of year when the plant flowers. A simple examination will show that at the end of each shoot, most woody plants have a 'growing point' in the form of a terminal or apical bud. Below this on the stem are arranged lateral or axillary buds in a characteristic formation, called phyllotaxis, which varies with the species concerned. Axillary buds derive their name from their point of origin on the plant; they form in the angle where a leaf is attached to the stem of the plant. This point is called the leaf axil, hence the buds are axillary buds. These buds may be arranged alternately, opposite, whorled or spirally, and their position will determine where the future side branches (lateral branches) are likely to develop.

The terminal bud exerts what is known as apical dominance over the axillary buds. In other words, it grows more rapidly and can assert dominance by producing chemicals which discourage the growth of the axillary buds. The axillary buds which are further away from the tip of a shoot or branch are less affected by these chemicals.

If the terminal bud is cut away or broken off, this chemical influence is eliminated, and the axillary buds or shoots respond by growing rapidly to form the lateral or side branches.

The degree of apical dominance varies considerably from one species of plant to another, and many plants display a more pronounced apical dominance when they are young, with this influence weakening as the plant ages.

Pruning Cuts (Positioning)

For plants where the buds are arranged alternately, any cut you make should be at an angle, 5mm (¼in) above a bud, with the bud itself near the high point of the cut. This is important because rapid healing is greatly influenced by the close proximity of the growth buds. It is usual to cut to an outward-pointing bud in order to encourage an open centre habit to the plant in bush roses, although with roses of spreading habit, it is sometimes useful to prune some branches to inward-pointing eyes to obtain more upright growth.

Wound Treatments

Whenever we make a pruning cut, there is a risk of decay developing within the wound and gradually invading the plant and eventually killing it. Historically, gardeners have been advised to use a wound paint on pruning cuts. Apparently, the Romans were the the first recorded users of protective coverings for pruning cuts. They used a compound called 'Noble Mummy', believed to have been a wax-like substance used in the mummification of bodies in Egypt. However, research over recent years now indicates that wound paints are not a very effective preventative measure in controlling diseases, and in some cases, may even encourage them by sealing the spores of infectious diseases into new wounds.

A misguided belief in the protective use of wound dressings has helped us to ignore the need to give the plant the best possible chance to use its own 'immune system' against the invasion of fungal decay. A woody plant has naturally occurring chemical and physical barriers within the wood which offer resistance to the invasion of rot-causing fungi. These barriers are most effective close to the point where a branch actually joins the main stem or trunk of a plant, and by making a good clean pruning cut at precisely the right point, we can give the plant the best opportunity possible to form these natural barriers.

This natural barrier point can easily be seen on many trees, as the area of slight swelling at the base of a branch. Arborists refer to it as the 'branch bark ridge', and

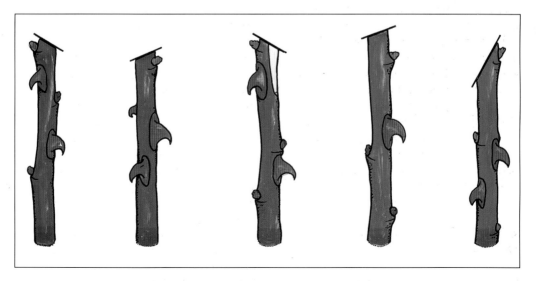

The two stems on the left have been pruned correctly. The three on the right are all examples of badly positioned cuts.

pruning at this point also appears to produce improved healing-over of the cut surfaces.

In America, Dr Alex Shigo of the United States Forestry Service, conducted extensive experiments over a seven-year period into the uses and effectiveness of wound treatments. He found no difference in the amount of decay in wounds which had been treated compared with those which had not.

His research indicated that wound dressings do not prevent or stop decay but are basically a cosmetic exercise. Pruning wounds, like any other injuries a plant might suffer, are possible entry points for disease, but the risk is reduced by making well-placed, clean cuts with sharp, well-maintained tools, used quickly and skillfully.

Most deciduous plants are best pruned either after they have finished flowering, or in the late autumn and winter when they are dormant. However, some species are pruned in full leaf to protect them from excessive 'bleeding'. *Acer* (Maple), *Aesculus* (Horse chestnut), *Betula* (Birch), *Juglans* (Walnut) and *Prunus* (Cherry) all exude large amounts of sap 'bleed' if pruned in the late winter or early spring. For this reason, they are pruned in the summer when the leaves have fully expanded and matured and are losing large quantities of water due to transpiration (evaporation). As the leaves 'pull' sap past the pruning wounds, they will remain relatively dry and hardly bleed.

Bark Ringing

Bark ringing is a very useful technique for special circumstances when the more usual methods of pruning have proved to be ineffective. If a few trees are grown, only one should be treated in the first instance and the effects monitored before ringing is carried out on the remaining plants.

In principle, this method consists of removing a complete strip of bark from the main trunk down to the cambium layer (the thin layer of cells on the surface of the wood).

This, in effect, becomes a restrictive barrier which checks the downward movement of carbohydrates and growth promoting chemicals; these then accumulate in the tissues above the ring. Thus, only that part of the tree below the ring is affected by the lack of foodstuffs and chemicals, root activity is slowed down, resulting in restricted top growth.

Root Pruning

Root pruning is sometimes used to control the vigour of trees and shrubs and to make them produce more flowers. It works because certain chemicals which occur in the roots of plants actually influence the rate of growth and spread of the branches. By removing sections of root the manufacture and supply of these chemicals (cytokinins) is restricted, which in turn has the effect of restricting the development and extension growth of the branches.

Stem Pruning

This can vary immensely; anything from pinching out soft sappy growth, or deadheading, through to branch removal or stooling (where all of the plant is cut to the ground annually).

Renewal Pruning

This method of pruning is based on a system of encouraging new side shoots to develop by removing the lateral branches on a regular basis. This is usually done straight after flowering.

Pinching Out (Stopping)

One of the main techniques used in shaping a plant is pinching out or stopping. This involves the removal of the growing point, to encourage the side shoots to develop. Usually this growth is snapped out using a finger and thumb because it is removed when it is very soft and sappy.

Dead-Heading

After flowering, the spent blooms can remain on the plant for several months. If the individual flowers have been pollinated a seed pod or hip will form. As the plant diverts much of its energy into forming seed, the tendency to produce flowers decreases, and eventually stops completely. The removal of the spent blooms stimulates the rapid development of another flush of flowers. When dead-heading, remove only the dead flower and it's supporting flower stalk, as this retains the maximum number of leaves to manufacture food for the plant.

Pollarding

This technique of hard pruning (used on trees and shrubs) is a traditional method of management designed to give a constant and renewable supply of shoots. Most of the plants are cut back regularly in the spring to within about 5–8cm (2–3in) of the main stem, which is anything up to 2m (6ft) above ground level. Vigorous shrubs such as *Salix alba* 'Chermesina' (Willow) can be pruned in this way to ensure a reliable display of highly attractive brightly coloured young shoots, which are more striking in the winter.

CHAPTER 2

Roses

The rose is by far the most popular hardy garden plant in the British Isles, due largely to the immense diversity of size, habit, shape, scent and colour which are available. Even those who declare themselves to be 'bad gardeners' usually grow at least one rose in their garden or against the walls of their house. Doubts over the wisdom of growing roses only tend to surface when we are faced with the task of pruning them properly, and for many, this remains a subject shrouded in myth and mystery.

In the wild, roses naturally produce strong new stems each season from close to the base of the plant. The water and nutrients taken up by the root system are thus directed to the new stems at the expense of the older, original stems which gradually become weaker and die as they are starved out. These old stems remain as dead wood before eventually rotting and falling to the ground. This is the closest the plants come to being pruned in nature and illustrates that, in effect, the plant does prune itself.

The purpose of pruning in an ornamental situation is to short-circuit nature by cutting out the older, less vigorous stems to encourage the production of strong and vigorous new growth, which is disease free and will produce the optimum number of flowers.

Pruning is actually a relatively simple operation. The complications arise because of the vast range roses cover with their different rates of growth and flowering habits. At one end of the spectrum are the patio and ground cover roses, many of which are 30cm (12in) tall or less, whilst at the other are the very vigorous climbers, ramblers and species roses, capable of reaching 10–15m (30–45ft) or more. A variety of techniques has to be used to meet the requirements of each individual species within this diverse group in order to keep them flowering, healthy, and under control (particularly the most vigorous ones).

GENERAL PRINCIPLES

There are certain basic principles which apply when pruning all types of rose:

1. Any cut you make should be at an angle, 5mm (¼in) above a bud, with the bud itself near the high point of the cut. This is important because rapid healing is greatly influenced by the close proximity of the growth buds.
2. Cut to an outward-pointing bud in order to encourage an open-centred habit in bush roses, although with roses of spreading habit it is sometimes useful to prune some branches to inward-pointing eyes to obtain more upright growth.
3. Cut back into healthy wood. If the middle of the stem is brown or discoloured, cut the shoot back further until healthy white wood is reached.
4. Completely remove any dead, damaged and diseased stems, and any weak or spindly growth. This will sometimes mean pruning stems to ground level or, with side shoots, cutting back to where they join a healthy stem.
5. Keep the centre of the plant open and clear of crossing branches and make sure that all the other branches are well

Bad pruning cuts usually lead to sections of the stem turning yellow and dying back. These sections of stem are ideal sites for disease to establish on the plant.

7. Always use sharp secateurs and knives, as a ragged cut caused by blunt tools leaves damaged tissue which is more susceptible to attack from pests and disease.

You may not know which group the roses in your garden belong to, particularly if you moved house in late autumn or winter and there are no labels on the plants. If you are not sure how to deal with them, confine your winter pruning to the points made under the general principles heading. Next summer you can see from the way they flower which group they belong to and prune accordingly. Pruning techniques may vary slightly in different conditions, but with experience you will quickly learn how to deal with them to suit your own local soil and microclimate.

The timing of pruning differs to some extent with the group of roses concerned and further details are given in each section.

Winter Pruning

Winter pruning is best carried out between mid-February and mid-March, depending on your location, and the prevailing weather conditions. Earlier pruning, from December to January can cause too much early growth which is often damaged by the weather. Later pruning, in April, often involves wasting the plant's energy by cutting off young growth it has already produced. The best guide is to prune, weather permitting, when the growth buds halfway up the most vigorous stems are beginning to swell.

Frost damage may occur in some seasons particularly with fluctuating spring weather where warm spells are followed by frosty periods. If the new shoots are damaged by frost, cut them back to the dormant buds further down the main stems.

Summer Pruning

Summer pruning is confined to the removal of flowers or flower clusters

spaced. This allows air to flow freely through the plant, and avoids the still air conditions which encourage fungal diseases such as black spot, mildew and rust. Spacing the branches prevents them rubbing together, which opens up wounds where other fungal problems such as coral spot can enter.

6. Collect and burn or shred all fallen leaves and prunings to reduce the risk of pests and diseases overwintering to return and attack again next year.

The early spring growth from the top bud can be killed by frost, this shoot should be cut back to the next live bud.

DEAD-HEADING

After flowering, the spent blooms can remain on the plant for several months if the individual flowers have been pollinated a seed pod or hip will form. As the plant diverts much of its energy into forming seed, the tendency to produce flowers decreases, and eventually stops completely. The removal of the spent blooms from

the plant stimulates the rapid development of another flush of flowers. When dead-heading, remove only the dead flower and its supporting flower stalk, as this retains the maximum number of leaves to manufacture food for the plant.

(dead-heading) to encourage the production of more flowers, and is carried out during the flowering season. Towards the end of the flowering period, it may be preferable to leave the dead flowers in place in order to allow hips to form to give some colour in autumn.

Autumn Pruning

In very windy areas, it is worth shortening any very long growths by 15–30cm (6–12in) during November. This lessens the risk of the wind rocking and loosening the plant.

MODERN ROSES

Most modern roses flower on the current season's wood, which means they need to be pruned quite severely in spring or they tend to become very tall and 'leggy' with the flowers forming high on the plant.

Ground Cover Types

Many of these plants such as 'Flower Carpet' will flower for many years with little or no formal pruning, and it is only necessary to cut out any dead, diseased or damaged stems. Often, the only planned pruning required is to dead-head, and to prevent them from spreading too far by cutting long shoots well back into their allotted area to an upward-facing bud.

Miniature Roses

These roses are not particularly vigorous, and the best approach is to give them only the minimum of attention by removing any shoots which have died back. Occasionally thin out the shoots of cultivars which have a tendency to produce a dense thicket of thin twiggy growth, and reduce the length of any over-vigorous shoots that throw the whole plant out of balance.

Hybrid Tea Types

Start by completely removing any dead, diseased, or damaged shoots, and the growth which is left will give you some indication of what you have to work with. Next, thin out any spindly, weak stems or shoots which are crossing the centre of the plant, the aim being to leave a well-balanced plant with good air circulation.

For older established bushes, cut out any thick stumps left from previous years, using long-handled loppers or a pruning saw. The remaining growth, consisting of the main stems, should then be cut back to 15cm (6in), if you want to rejuvenate the plant, but to two or three buds if you want large flowers. However, you will need to bear in mind that these larger blooms will often be

---

TOPPING

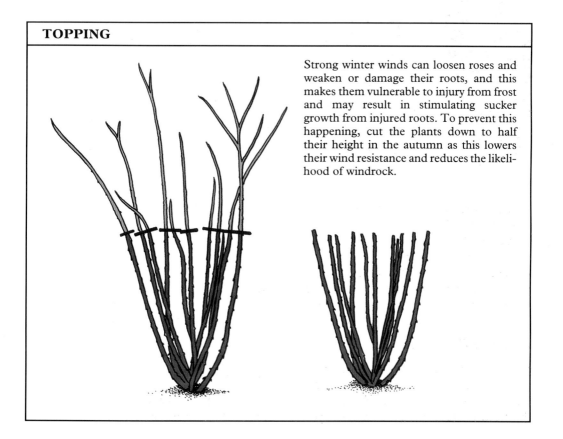

Strong winter winds can loosen roses and weaken or damage their roots, and this makes them vulnerable to injury from frost and may result in stimulating sucker growth from injured roots. To prevent this happening, cut the plants down to half their height in the autumn as this lowers their wind resistance and reduces the likelihood of windrock.

PRUNING HYBRID TEA TYPES

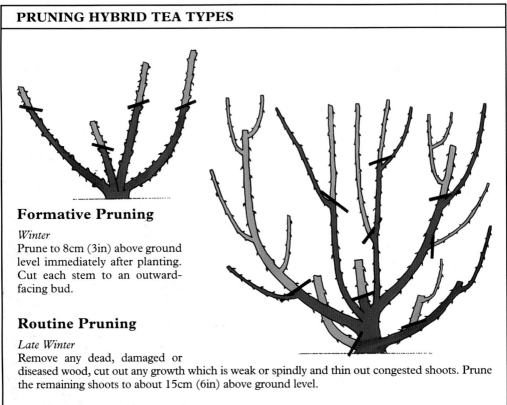

Formative Pruning

Winter
Prune to 8cm (3in) above ground level immediately after planting. Cut each stem to an outward-facing bud.

Routine Pruning

Late Winter
Remove any dead, damaged or diseased wood, cut out any growth which is weak or spindly and thin out congested shoots. Prune the remaining shoots to about 15cm (6in) above ground level.

Dead-head the spent blooms as they appear.

---

produced about three weeks late as a result of this severe pruning. A useful tip with bedding roses is to prune half of the plants in the usual way, and the remaining plants hard to stagger the start of the flowering period and extend the flowering season: this is referred to as 'relay pruning'.

Floribunda Types

As with the large-flowered bush type, remove any dead, diseased, or damaged shoots and the growth which is left will give you some indication of what you have to work with. With lower-growing cultivars, prune the main stems down to 20–25cm (8–10in) and all the side shoots back by about a third. For the taller cultivars, such as 'Chinatown', both the main stems and the side shoots are reduced to about one third of their original length.

Pruning Floribunda Types
Over the past few years, the Royal National Rose Society have conducted a series of pruning trials on hybrid tea and floribunda-type roses. The results have shown that roses pruned by simply cutting off the top 30 per cent of growth with an electric hedge trimmer gave a better display and more blooms than roses that were pruned in the more conventional manner. This appears to indicate that modern roses are much tougher and more resilient than previously imagined. These trials are ongoing with new information being released regularly.

PRUNING FLORIBUNDA TYPES

Formative Pruning

Winter
Prune to 8cm (3in) above ground level immediately after planting. Cut each stem to an outward-facing bud.

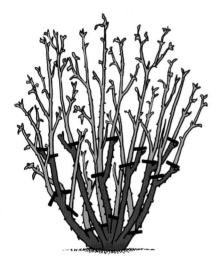

Routine pruning

Late winter
Remove any dead, damaged or diseased wood, cut out any growth which is weak or spindly and thin out congested shoots. Prune the remaining shoots to about 20–25cm (8–10in) above ground level.

Dead-head the spent blooms as they appear.

Shrub, Species and Old Garden Roses

Although this covers a large and varied group of roses, all of the species and most of the shrub roses both old and modern,

A well-pruned species rose, in early spring.

Shrub roses need to be trimmed back by about one-third of their extension growth.

flower on wood which is two years or more in age. Many will flower freely for a number of years without any formal pruning.

When they are pruned, start by removing all of the weak, dead, damaged and diseased wood. Follow with only a light pruning to leave as much flower-bearing wood as possible. This is particularly important for those roses which are repeat flowering. The best approach is to completely remove two or three of the oldest stems each year, so that over a three or four year period, all of the growth is gradually renewed. A form of annual renewal pruning would be the most accurate description of this pruning method.

The best time for this method of pruning is immediately after flowering, as this gives the plant the chance to channel its energy into the development of new stems. The main exceptions within this broad grouping would be those species such as *Rosa rugosa, Rosa moyesii* and their respective hybrids, which are valued for their attractive display of hips, and these should be pruned in late winter.

Climbing and Rambling Roses

These roses require minor pruning but regular annual training. Neither are self-supporting and, if not given the correct training, they will not flower freely and may become bare at the base.

Climbing Roses
In their first year (and also the second unless they have made exceptional growth) do not prune climbing roses except to remove any dead, diseased, damaged or weak growth. Never prune climbing sports of bush roses (roses with the word 'climbing' before the cultivar name, for example 'Climbing Peace') in the first two years, because they may revert to the bush form if cut back hard too soon.

You can begin training, however, as soon as the new shoots are long enough

A climbing rose with its growth trained horizontally to encourage the development of more flowers.

A climbing rose showing how the stems gradually become bare at the base (opposite).

Prune climbing roses after flowering, cut out very old stems, reduce the side-shoots back to five buds, and tie in new growths.

to reach their supports. Training them sideways along horizontal supports will encourage flowering, but where this is not possible, such as on a narrow area between a door and a window, choose a cultivar that is halfway between a tall shrub and a climbing rose, such as 'Golden Showers' or 'Joseph's Coat'. Many of these will produce flowers from the base of the plant without any special training.

Many climbing roses flower well for years with nothing other than general pruning, done in the autumn after flowering. Leave the strong main shoots unpruned, unless they are exceeding their allotted space, in which case shorten them as appropriate. Otherwise, simply shorten the side shoots. Train in all the new season's growth to the supports while it is still flexible.

Occasional renewal pruning may be necessary if the base of a climbing rose becomes very bare. Cut back one or two of the older, main shoots to within 15cm (6in) or so of ground level to encourage vigorous, new

shoots to develop and replace the older growths. This process should be repeated as required in subsequent years.

Rambling Roses

Rambling roses will flower quite satisfactorily for many years with no formal pruning, but if they are not carefully trained, they will grow into a tangle of unmanageable and unhealthy shoots. This is because they produce much more growth from the base than most climbers, which results in poor air circulation, and encourages the incidence of fungal diseases such as black spot, mildew and rust. This dense bushy growth also makes it very difficult to spray the plants thoroughly to control these diseases or pests such as greenfly.

The best time to prune rambling roses is in late summer. For the first two years, pruning should be limited to removing all dead, damaged or diseased wood, and cutting back any side shoots to within 7.5cm (3in) of a vigorous shoot. From the third

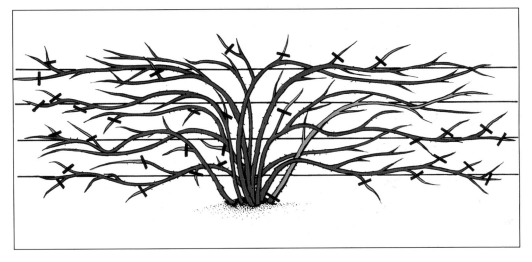

Ramblers are pruned soon after flowering. Cut the side-shoots back to five buds. Cut out any old stems, and tie-in the rest.

year onwards, prune the rose more severely in order to maintain a framework. After removing all dead, damaged or diseased wood, cut out 25–30 per cent of the oldest shoots, leaving only vigorous new stems and strong, healthy two-year-old growth. Finally, cut back any side shoots to two or three buds.

Standard Roses

Most standard roses have an extended rootstock stem which is budded or grafted with a bush variety at 1.1–1.2m (3½–4ft) above soil level. Weeping standard roses have a rambling rose cultivar budded or grafted onto a stem at 1.5–1.8m (5–6ft) above soil level.

The pruning of the 'head' of the standard will be the same as for those plants budded or grafted at ground level, and it is still important to keep an even and balanced arrangement of branches. The main difference in pruning is in the timing as standards are much more susceptible to wind damage

Prune standards in the autumn by thinning out the branches and reducing all other stems by one-third.

during the winter months. Pruning in the autumn soon after leaf-fall reduces the wind resistance of the 'head' which helps to decrease wind-rock damage to the stem and roots of the plant.

RENOVATION PRUNING

Left to their own devices, roses which are neglected and left unpruned will often flower for many years, but before too long they are usually in a pretty sorry state. Eventually, the plant becomes a tangled mass of dead stems and diseased leaves with small, badly-shaped flowers. Most roses need pruning to stay healthy, vigorous and free flowering, and although a few vigorous rambling species such as *Rosa wichuriana*

perform very well for many years without any attention, these are the exceptions.

Fortunately, most roses are very tough and will respond well to severe pruning, an extreme treatment which can rejuvenate some of the most seemingly hopeless cases of neglect, although there are always some roses which cannot tolerate this horticultural savagery. The usual response of the plant is to produce a plentiful supply of strong new stems, but sometimes a proportion of this growth is from the rootstock and

---

STEPS TO RECLAIM AN OLD PLANT

1. In the first winter, all of the dead, diseased and damaged wood is cut out to ground level. Then completely remove (to ground level) half of the live stems and, finally, cut all side shoots on the remaining stems back to three or four buds.

2. The following winter, all of the old stems which were not cut out the previous year are now removed. The new stems which have developed may need thinning out to prevent overcrowding, and finally on the remaining new stems, cut all side shoots back to three or four buds.

1.

3. By year three, it should be impossible to tell how badly neglected the plant was before you started the whole process.

2.

3.

BARK RINGING

Before starting it helps if the cause for this undesirably excessive growth is identified. The main factors which contribute to this problem are:

a. over-vigorous rootstocks, the wrong type of root-stock on trees or shrubs which have been budded or grafted,

b. high rainfall during the growing season,

c. very fertile soils,

d. excessive feeding (especially Nitrogen),

e. the heavy application of organic mulches.

1. Wrap a strip of tape around the stem of the plant (this will act as a guide for cutting).

2. Make two parallel cuts into the bark (press the knife in until you feel the firmness of the wood beneath), make these cuts around the entire circumference of the stem.

3. Using the tip of a knife carefully lift out the strip of bark isolated between the two cuts.

4. Cover the open wound with a strip of electricians' insulation tape.

5. By late summer when the wound has healed the tape can be removed.

This process should only be carried out once a year, but there is no limit to the number of years a plant can be bark-ringed.

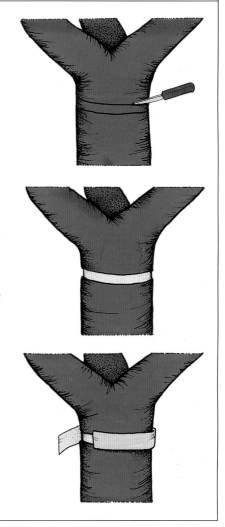

some work has to be done in order to check and remove these suckers.

In addition, the production of an excess of vigorous growth may lead to a high proportion of 'blind shoots', which have no growing point and do not produce flowers. These should be cut back to half of their original length to encourage new growth and flowers.

Often, it is better to play safe and renovate the neglected plants over a number of years. Even the worst cases of neglect usually a have a few younger more vigorous stems which should be kept if possible.

Sucker Removal

This should be carried out as a matter of course whenever suckers occur, but pruning involves a close inspection of the plant and how well it is growing, and is a good time to check to find any which might have been missed during the growing season.

Remove suckers as close to the point of origin as possible.

Suckers are actually shoots produced by the rootstock onto which a variety has been budded or grafted, and are usually much more vigorous. They usually emerge through the soil from below the bud union, with leaves and stems of a much lighter green than those of the variety, and usually more leaflets per whole 'leaf'.

Some rootstocks produce suckers more readily than others. They mostly occur when the rose has been planted too deeply (because the variety tries to form its own root system), or if the roots have been damaged in some way, e.g. by hoeing too deeply (which triggers a natural response to form shoots).

Suckers compete with the main plant for water, light and nutrients, but because they have a faster growth rate, the rootstock growth usually wins. As this will eventually kill the variety, it is essential that they are removed as soon as possible.

Remove by carefully digging the soil from around the base of the sucker with a trowel, to find where the sucker is attached to the plant. Then, wearing a glove for protection, tear the sucker away by hand. This will rip out not only the sucker stem, but also all the dormant buds around its base.

Shoots which develop below the bud union on the stem of a standard rose are also suckers (they still originate from the rootstock), and these should also be torn off the stem by hand to remove all the dormant buds around their bases.

Cutting off suckers has a pruning effect and usually leads to more suckers developing from buds left beneath the cut.

ROSE PRUNING (SEASONAL GUIDE)

SUBJECT	PRUNING TIME	RESPONSE TO RENOVATION
Low-growing roses(ground cover type)	early spring (no regular pruning)	√
Miniature roses	early spring (no regular pruning)	X
Large-flowered (hybrid tea type)	early spring	√
Cluster-Flowered (floribunda type)	early spring	√
Shrub, species and old garden roses	after flowering late winter (cultivars with ornamental hips)	√
Climbing roses	autumn, soon after flowering	√
Rambling roses	late summer, soon after flowering	√
Standard roses	late autumn early winter	X

CHAPTER 3

Climbing and Wall Plants

Walls, fences and other upright structures provide a multitude of suitable positions for supporting a wide range of climbing plants and trained shrubs. In most gardens, you will find a climbing rose or a clematis growing against the house, but it is rare for an available wall or fence space to be used to its true potential.

Any upright structure, regardless of aspect, has the potential to be a support for tall or upright plants, providing the opportunity to create a vertical garden. Climbing plants and wall shrubs make an immediate visual impact and soon hide, or at least disguise, some of their support. Many of the plants used provide strong colour, or are capable of a more subtle softening effect by breaking up the rigid uniform lines of a building.

Walls and fences also provide shelter for slightly tender plants which are not fully frost-hardy in the open garden. Additional vertical growing space can be created by means of pergolas, arbours, pillars and other devices or allowing climbers to scramble through trees or hedges.

Climbers pruned and trained over an arch.

BASIC PRINCIPLES

Routine pruning is essential for the successful cultivation of almost all established
climbers. Without this control, the plants
eventually produce only a sparse display of
flowers. More importantly, some of the
most vigorous climbers may engulf neighbouring plants, and damage roofs, gutters,
and masonry. Training may be combined
with pruning to achieve the most desirable
structure and appearance of the plant.

When pruning climbers and wall shrubs,
the operation of pruning is usually closely
linked to training and support. Training is
aimed at guiding a selected number of
strong, healthy stems onto and over the
support framework while they are supple
enough to create the desired shape.

Some climbers, such as *Fallopia aubertii*,
and *F. baldschuanicum* (Russian vines) produce masses of long slender shoots in addition to the main stems, and these frequently
need to be tied to the support during training to retain the required shape. Usually,
vigorous climbers are quite difficult to train,
and after the first year or so they are best left
to grow freely, often being pruned only
when they grow beyond their allocated area.

When considering the pruning of the
many plants which can be used in these
positions, it is important to bear in mind
that the growth habits and details of basic
cultivation can influence the training and
subsequent pruning of both climbers and
wall shrubs.

The plants used can be divided into various groups based on their growth habit.

1. The natural **clingers**, such as *Hedera*
   (ivy) and *Parthenocissus* (Virginia creep-
   er), which support themselves by aerial
   roots or sucker pads. Usually no additional support system is needed.
2. The **twiners**, a large group including
   Lonicera (honeysuckle), *Clematis* and *Wisteria*, which climb by means of rapidly

A display of seed heads from a Clematis *trained
over a pergola.*

growing stems, which are then supported
by curling or twining tendrils, leaf-stalks
or stems. A support system is usually
required.
3. The **scramblers** and **ramblers**, rapidly growing stems which clamber through
   other plants in the wild using hooked
   thorns (roses) or by rapid extension of
   lax shoots *Pyracantha* (Firethorn). A
   support system is needed to which they
   can be tied.
4. Shrubs which are tender enough to
   require the protection of a wall or fence.

They may either grow next to a wall or fence, or be supported by it, depending upon the plant grown.

CLIMBERS

True climbers have their own method of self-support, and most usually require routine training and pruning once they are established. Without this regular attention, many plants will direct most of their energy into extension growth, and often flower poorly. Training and pruning are usually combined operations for this type of plant. Often the key to correct pruning is based on the flowering period, and method of self-support.

Formative Pruning and Training

Soon after planting, as the new extension growth begins, the training of wall shrubs and climbers consists of placing and tying in the strongest stems to the support system to achieve a well-spaced, balanced framework of shoots.

During the growing season, climbers that have their own methods of support may need to be 'coaxed' into growing in the desired direction. Temporarily fixing them in place while they are still soft and pliable and until the twining stems or tendrils attach themselves to their support is often a good idea. The woody stems which develop as the shoot becomes mature cannot be bent into the required position without damaging them.

In the second spring after the plant has established, cut back all of the side shoots to a bud that is close to the main stem and tie in the pruned shoots to the support system. A number of strong stems will grow from these shoots during the following season, forming the framework of the plant. Train these shoots as they develop.

The following year, cut back each stem to a bud pointing in the direction in which the stem is intended to be trained. This provides vigorous shoots which develop to extend the main branch framework. Carefully tie in all the stems, or encourage them to gain a grip by their own devices. Cut back any other shoots to within two buds of the nearest stem.

Clematis

The *Clematis* is quite rightly called the queen of climbers. It has the longest flowering period of any climber, the different species and cultivars offering a selection to provide flowers for most months of the year.

Pruning requirements vary depending on which variety is grown, and although, over the years, a great deal of myth has developed around

SELF-SUPPORTING CLIMBERS	
PLANT NAME	METHOD OF SUPPORT
Akebia	
Lonicera (Honeysuckle)	twining stems
Wisteria	
Clematis	
Eccremocarpus	
(Chilean Glory Flower)	twining leaf stalks
Tropaeolum	
Campsis (Trumpet Vine)	
Hedera (Ivy)	aerial roots
Hydrangea petiolaris	
Ampelopsis	
Passiflora (Passion Flower)	tendrils
Vitis (Vine)	
Parthenocissus (Boston Ivy)	sucker pads

PRUNING AND TRAINING

Formative Pruning

First Year

Winter
After planting, as the new growth begins, place and tie the strongest stems into the support system. Prune back side shoots to promote new growth.

Spring
Cut back all side shoots close to the main stem, and tie them to the support system to form the framework of the plant. Remove any frost-damaged growth.

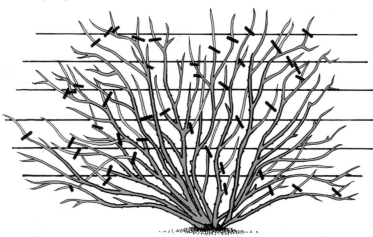

Summer
Climbers with their own support methods need 'coaxing' to grow in the desired direction.

Second Year

Summer
Cut back each stem to provide vigorous shoots which will extend the main branch framework. Tie in all stems, or encourage them to gain a grip by their own devices. Cut back any unwanted shoots to two buds.

clematis pruning, it is a topic which can be very effectively simplified.

The key to pruning is really when the flowering season occurs.

Group One – Those which Flower from January through to late May
Many of the *Clematis* in this group are quite vigorous and require little routine pruning.

Because they are vigorous, it may be necessary to prune them in order to keep them tidy or to prevent them from spreading beyond their allotted space. If this is the case, the best time for any pruning to be done is immediately after flowering. This gives the maximum possible time for the new growth to develop and ripen during the late summer and autumn so the plant will flower as usual the following spring.

Any growths which are surplus to requirements may be cut back in the autumn, but this will reduce the number of flowers the following spring. *C. armandii* responds better to having the older stems pruned (thinned out) in rotation, to avoid congestion. These should be cut back to strong, young shoots immediately after flowering.

Group One – Early-Flowering Species
    Clematis alpina and cvs
    Clematis armandii and cvs
    Clematis cirrhosa and cvs
    Clematis macropetala and cvs
    Clematis montana and cvs

PRUNING *CLEMATIS* GROUP ONE

Formative Pruning

First Year

Spring
Cut back all stems to a pair of buds at 30cm (1ft) above ground level.

Second Year

Spring
Cut back all stems to a pair of buds at 1m (3ft) above ground level.

Routine Pruning

Spring
The best time for pruning is immediately after flowering. Evergreen clematis respond better to having older stems thinned out.

PRUNING *CLEMATIS* GROUP TWO

Formative Pruning

First Year

Spring
Cut back all stems to a pair of buds at 30cm (1ft) above ground level.

Second Year

Spring
Cut back all stems to a pair of buds at 1m (3ft) above ground level.

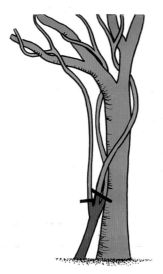

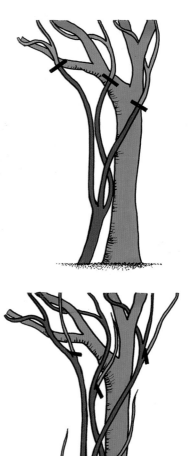

Routine Pruning

Spring
Prune just before the new growth starts, remove the dead, weak, or damaged stems. Cut back healthy stems just above a pair of buds.

Group Two – Those which Flower from early June through to early July
The large, single flowers are produced on stems of varying lengths up to 60cm (2ft) which arise from the previous season's ripened stems. Prune these plants in the early spring just before the new growth fully commences. Remove any dead, weak, or damaged growth and cut back healthy stems to just above a strong pair of leaf buds. It is these buds which will produce the main flower display.

Clematis in this group often produce a second flush of blooms on new shoots in late summer. This habit can be exploited by the gardener by pruning half of the shoots much harder in the spring to encourage a more prominent later flush of flowers, and so extend the flowering season; this is known as 'relay pruning', and was regularly practised by Victorian gardeners.

Group Two – Early Large-Flowered Cultivars
    Clematis 'Barbara Jackman'
    Clematis 'Carnaby'
    Clematis 'Daniel Deronda'
    Clematis 'Duchess of Edinburgh'
    Clematis 'Elsa Spath'
    Clematis 'General Sikorski'
    Clematis 'Henryii'
    Clematis 'Lasurstern'
    Clematis 'Marie Boisselot'
    Clematis 'Mrs N. Thompson'
    Clematis 'Nelly Moser'
    Clematis 'Niobe'
    Clematis 'The President'
    Clematis 'Vyvyan Pennell'

PRUNING *CLEMATIS* GROUP THREE

Formative Pruning

Spring
Cut back all stems to a pair of buds at 30cm (1ft) above ground level.

Routine Pruning

Spring
Prune back all stems to within 45cm (18in) of soil level, usually just above the start of the previous season's growth.

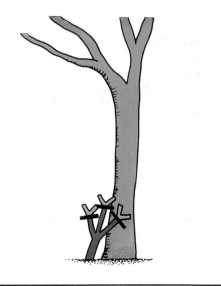

Group Three – Those which Flower from early July through to October

This group produces flowers on stems of the current season's growth and should be pruned in the early spring before new growth starts. Remove all of the previous season's growth by cutting to a strong pair of buds within 45cm (18in) of soil level. As new growth appears, train it into its support, so the tendrils can take over support.

In the spring, great care must be taken as the new stems are brittle and easily snapped. Space the shoots evenly and tie them in at regular intervals.

Group Three – Late-Flowering Species and Cultivars

  Clematis florida and cvs
  Clematis tangutica and cvs
  Clematis viticella and cvs
  Clematis 'Comtesse de Bouchaud'
  Clematis 'Duchess of Albany'
  Clematis 'Ernest Markham'
  Clematis 'Gipsy Queen'
  Clematis 'Hagley Hybrid'
  Clematis × 'Jackmanii'
  Clematis 'Lady Betty Balfour'
  Clematis 'Perle d'Azure'
  Clematis 'Ville de Lyon'

Wisteria floribunda, *regularly pruned, rewards you with a dramatic flower display.*

Wisteria

This outstanding climber leaves some gardeners shivering with fear at the thought of attempting to prune it. The key is to check the production of strong vigorous shoots so that more of the plant's energy is directed into flower production. The flower buds are produced on short spurs of growth, and more spurs are produced on branches which are trained horizontally.

Routine Pruning

With established plants, the easiest approach is simply to prune them twice each year.

The first pruning is carried out in the summer, when the new long lateral growths are cut back to just above a bud 15–20cm (6–8in), from the point where they emerge from the stem. Any shoots intended to be used as part of the plant's framework are tied into position and left to twine around the supports.

WISTERIA

Formative Pruning

First Year

Spring
Remove any growth damaged by frost or wind, and prune back the tip of each shoot to a strong healthy bud.

Summer
Train in the young growths as they develop, and prune back the tip of any excessively vigorous shoots.

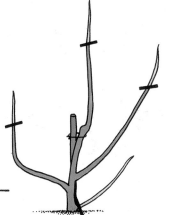

Second Year

Spring
Remove any growth damaged by frost or wind, and prune back the tip of each shoot to a strong, healthy bud. Train some shoots into a horizontal position.

Summer
Train in the young growths as they develop, and prune back the tip of any excessively vigorous shoots to 20cm (8in).

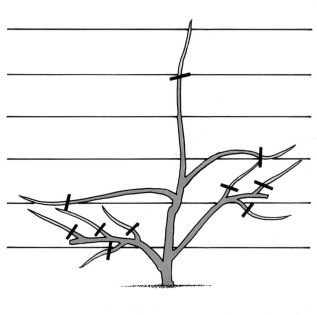

WISTERIA – ROUTINE PRUNING

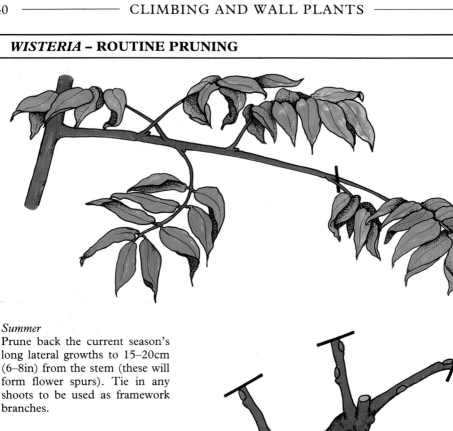

Summer
Prune back the current season's long lateral growths to 15–20cm (6–8in) from the stem (these will form flower spurs). Tie in any shoots to be used as framework branches.

Winter
Cut back all summer-pruned shoots consisting of two or three strong buds, which carry the flowers. Any secondary growths are cut back to 15–20cm (6–8in).

The second pruning is carried out in late winter, when all of the summer pruned shoots are cut back to form spurs consisting of two or three strong buds, which carry the flowers. At the same time, any secondary growths which formed after the summer pruning are cut back to 15–20cm (6–8in).

Renovation Pruning
Neglected climbers soon become a tangled mass of woody stems, and produce very few flowers. If the plant is healthy and vigorous, the best approach is to prune it very hard to rejuvenate it. Most climbers will tolerate being cut back close to the base or back to the main framework of stems.

The first step is to cut down the plant to 30cm (12in) tall in the early spring. As the new growth develops, it can then be trained over the support system. Applying a top dressing of fertilizer, and watering it in well, will help to promote the rapid growth of new shoots.

Those plants which are not healthy and vigorous may not survive such harsh treatment, and if this is the case, it is advisable to carry out the renovation pruning in stages over a two- or three-year period. Remove the oldest stems each year (usually the darkest coloured bark).

Renovating plants over several years is made more difficult as the new growth which has been stimulated may become entangled with the old shoots which are to be removed later. To avoid this, in the first year, only cut down one side of the plant and train the new shoots into the open spaces created by removing the unwanted growths. The remainder of the old stems are cut away in the second year and replacements trained into the remaining space. Be prepared to wait for two or more years before the new growth is mature enough to produce flowers.

On old, neglected, or straggly wall shrubs, severe pruning can be practised. Most will respond well, and usually produce plenty of vigorous young growth from the base. Not all shrubs will take kindly to this treatment, for example *Cytisus* (broom) will die rather than produce new growths when pruned in this way, and not even pruning in stages will stimulate new growth.

PRUNING CLIMBERS AND WALL SHRUBS (SEASONAL GUIDE)

SUBJECT	PRUNING TIME	RESPONSE TO RENOVATION
Abelia grandiflora	early spring	√
Abutilon megapotanicum	mid–late spring	√
Actinidia kolomikta	early spring	√
Camellia × williamsii cvs	none	X
Campsis species	autumn	√
Ceanothus species	after flowering	√
Celastrus orbiculatus	after fruiting	√
Chaenomeles species	midsummer	√
Clematis species and cvs	see above	√
Cytisus battandieri	after flowering if required	X
Desfontainia spinosa	none required	X
Escallonia species	after flowering	√
Fallopia species	early spring if required	√
Garrya elliptica	after flowering if required	√
Hydrangea petiolaris	none required	X
Jasminum nudiflorum	after flowering	√
Lonicera species	early spring	√
Parthenocissus henryana	none required	√
Passiflora species	early spring	√
Pyracantha species and cvs	midsummer	√
Solanum crispum	early spring	√
Wisteria sinensis	after flowering and early spring	√

WISTERIA – RENOVATION PRUNING

First Year

Spring
Cut all stems back to 30cm (12in).

Summer/Autumn
Train and loosely tie in the new shoots as they develop.

Second Year

Untie all of the new stems, cut out all thin, weak or damaged growth. Thin out any overcrowded shoots, re-tie the remaining shoots to form a structural framework of branches.

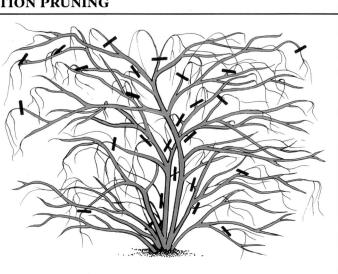

Climbers which Tolerate Renovation Pruning

Allamanda cathartica
Anredera cordifolia
Antigonon leptopus
Aristolochia
Campsis species and cvs
Clematis (most species)
Clerodendrum thomsoniae
Fallopia baldschuanicum
Lonicera (most species)
Passiflora (most species)
Vitis (most species)

EVERGREEN CLIMBERS AND WALL SHRUBS

These are best pruned in the early spring, late enough to avoid the dangers of frost damage but just before the plants start their surge of new growth.

Those evergreen plants which are grown for their

Fremontodendron *can be damaged by frost and needs pruning in late spring.*

Pyracantha. *The new growth should be pruned back as the berries start to change colour from green to orange.*

ROUTINE PRUNING
(*PYRACANTHA*)

Summer
Prune back the new growths to 10cm (4in)
of the lateral shoots.

Winter
Remove old fruit-bearing stalks when the
berries have finished. Prune back any
excessively vigorous growths which are
not required or spoil the overall balance of
the plant.

ROUTINE PRUNING
(*CEANOTHUS*)

Spring/Summer
Cut out the old flower bearing spurs to
within 10cm (4in) of the main stem.

Autumn
Prune back any excessively vigorous
growths which are not required or spoil
the overall balance of the plant.

flowers, in addition to their year-round
foliage, often produce flowers on the previous year's wood, and these should not be
pruned until after flowering e.g. *Clematis
armandii*.

Regardless of when the plant is pruned,
the work usually involves simply removing
dead or damaged wood and cutting back
stray shoots to retain the plant's shape. Any
long shoots which are to be kept should
also be tied in. A slight complication can
occur with plants which are grown for their
ornamental display of fruits, such as *Pyracantha* (Firethorn), where most of the new
growth appears in June and July, after flowering. This new growth often obscures the
berries, so to avoid this, the main time for

pruning mature plants is in midsummer,
when these new growths are pruned back to
within 10cm (4in) of the main stem. These
10cm (4in) shoots form spurs which will
bear next year's flowers. *Ceanothus* (Cali-
fornian lilac) is also pruned immediately
after flowering, but in this instance, the old
flower-bearing spurs are cut to within
10cm (4in) of the main stem, to encourage
the development of flower shoots for next
year.

The deciduous *Ceanothus* (*C.* 'Gloire de
Versailles' is possibly the best known) are
mainly summer and autumn flowering
plants. They can be pruned at the same
time as the evergreen cultivars, because
they flower on the current season's growth.

CHAPTER 4

Shrubs

There are a number of shrubs which make excellent garden plants without ever needing to be pruned or at most, having only a light trim. They are usually broad-leaved evergreens such as *Cotoneaster conspicuus*, *Ruscus aculeatus* and *Sarcococca humilis*. However, with their neat compact habit, they are the exception. They often require no more than the removal of dead, damaged, and diseased wood, and perhaps 'dead-heading' to remove the old stalks which have carried flowers and berries.

By far the greater number, if left to grow naturally, eventually become unattractive and deteriorate over a period of time as the overall growth suffers, and the health of the shrub declines. This is part of the plant's natural life cycle and not a cause for alarm. It may take many years to happen, depending to a large extent on the shrub and it's life expectancy. A regime of pruning regularly, or a combination of pruning and training will allow most shrubs to grow and flower well over a long period, and in many respects correct pruning on a regular basis can actually extend the fruitful life of the plant.

REASONS FOR PRUNING

In the early stages of a shrub's life, the main reason for pruning is to create a structural framework of branches as the basis for a vigorous, well-shaped plant. This process is known as **'formative'** pruning. Most shrubs also need pruning to sustain or improve the quality of their fruit, flowers, leaves or stems, and this is known as

'maintenance' or **'routine'** pruning. Certain **'renovation'** pruning techniques can also be used as a method of rejuvenating plants which have become neglected and overgrown, restoring them to good health and keeping them to a manageable size.

Whether or not the plant in question warrants being rescued is a matter of opinion by the individual on the spot. Harsh though it may seem, replacement is often the best course of action when a shrub requires regular cutting back because it is too large for the space available. In reality what you are dealing with is not a question of pruning, but more a question of poor plant selection when the plant was chosen for that particular spot.

DEAD OR ALIVE?

In the spring if a shrub appears to be dead, e.g. *Hibiscus syriacus* is very late coming into leaf, cut and peel back a small sliver of bark to see if there are any signs of life. A layer of green wood beneath the bark is a good sign, but if the wood is brown, you can be fairly sure that the branch in question is dead. Always err on the side of caution though, as some shrubs may remain dormant for a whole growing season.

TRAINING

Most shrubs grown in the open require pruning on a regular basis, but very little training at all, and it is only when plants are grown against supports that the gardener plays an active role in directing their growth. In these very artificial situations, plants normally require a combination of pruning and training to form a well-spaced framework of branches, and grow in a very precise way.

For example, the growth and development of lower buds or shoots on a stem may be varied by training. When stems are trained into a horizontal position, it causes a redistribution of the growth-promoting chemicals in the branch, and the lower shoots and buds grow more vigorously. Training branches horizontally can substantially increase the amount of flower and fruit a shrub will carry. Where no training is practised, and the stem is allowed to grow upright, lower shoots on the stem usually grow weakly. Trained shrubs should be tied into their supports as the growth develops, because the stems become far less flexible as they ripen and turn woody.

PRINCIPLES OF PRUNING AND TRAINING

The most common outcome of pruning is the production of vegetative or shoot growth, after all that is one of the reasons we prune in the first place. The apical bud (growing point) of a stem is usually chemically dominant over the growth buds immediately below it. This is often referred to as apical dominance, where the production of lateral shoots (side shoots) is suppressed by the chemicals produced in or close to this apical bud. Pruning to remove the tips of shoots leads to a chemical response within the plant, resulting in the development of more vigorous growth buds or, flowering shoots further back down the stem.

SEVERITY OF PRUNING

As the influence of the apical bud diminishes the further down the stem you cut, hard pruning promotes more vigorous growth than light pruning. Hard cutting back of a vigorous shoot often stimulates even stronger growth. 'Prune weak growth hard but prune strong growth only lightly' is an adage to bear in mind when attempting to correct the appearance of a misshapen shrub.

POSITIONING CUTS

Stems should be cut 2–3mm (about ⅛in) above a healthy bud. Select an appropriately placed bud facing the direction in which you want the new shoot to develop. As the shoot grows, it can be tied in to form part of a branch framework or be used to replace an old shoot.

Pruning cuts must be clean, with no crushing of the tissue or ragged edges, and at an angle slanting slightly away from the bud to reduce the risk of secondary damage from disease infection. The position of the cut is very important. Cuts which are made too close to the bud may cause damage to it, whereas one made too far away from the bud will leave a stub which is prone to die-back and could become an entry point for pests and disease.

HOW TO PRUNE

The cuts made when pruning create wounds, which are just like any other injuries a shrub might suffer, in that they are potential entry points for disease. Historically, gardeners have been advised to use a wound paint on pruning cuts, but recent research now indicates that wound paints are not a very effective preventative measure in controlling diseases and, in some cases, may even encourage them by sealing the spores of infectious diseases into new wounds. By making well-placed, clean cuts with sharp tools, this risk is reduced but never fully eliminated.

A poor pruning cut which has started to rot, possibly as a result of using a wound paint.

WOUND SEALANTS

Traditionally, 'wound paints' with a fungicidal property have been used to seal large wounds. However recent research suggests that these paints can seal fungal spores into the wound and actually encourage the establishment of fungus within the fresh wounds. In order to reduce the risk of infection to a minimum always use clean, sharp knives and secateurs to make clean cuts.

For shrubs with leaves in opposite pairs, cut at right angles straight across the shoot just above a pair of healthy buds. If both buds develop, this results in a forked branch system, and the weaker of the two buds will need removing as they develop. For stems with an alternate or whorled arrangement of leaves, make a slanting cut just above a bud, but not so close as to damage the bud.

Formative Pruning

The objective of formative pruning is to produce a framework of well-spaced branches so that the shrub can develop as closely as possible to its natural habit. How much formative pruning each shrub requires varies greatly, and depends on a number of factors, such as:

1. the type of shrub
2. its natural growth habit
3. the quality of the plants purchased.

DECIDUOUS SHRUBS

Deciduous shrubs are more likely to require formative pruning than evergreen ones. It should be done in the dormant season, between mid-autumn and mid-spring, at the time of planting, or soon after. As a general guide; if an over-vigorous shoot distorts the framework, cut it back lightly rather than severely; if there is no balanced branch framework, cut the plant back hard to promote strong new shoots; remove any spindly or crossing branches.

There are four basic groups:
1. those that require little or no pruning
2. those which flower on current season's growth and are pruned in the spring
3. those which flower usually on the previous seasons wood, and are pruned in the summer after flowering
4. those of suckering habit.

Formative pruning is essential to provide a sound structural framework for the shrub.

Other significant factors are the shrub's ability to produce replacement growth and the age of the flower-bearing wood.

Shrubs which Require Little or No Pruning

If a shrub does not produce vigorous shoots from the base or branches from the lower third of the stems on a regular basis, then it will need little pruning. Common exceptions to this rule are *Aralia chinensis* and *Rhus hirta*, both of which need very little pruning but often sucker profusely from the roots, up to 2–3m (6–9ft) away from the main stem.

The main requirement is simply to remove dead, diseased, or damaged wood to protect the overall health of the plant, and to cut out weak or crossing growth, ideally just after flowering. For shrubs in this group, formative pruning should be done on an ongoing basis, rather than just in the first few years after planting. Any shrubs such as Japanese maples, which are prone to heavy bleeding if pruned in late spring, should be pruned in mid-to late summer, when their sap is not flowing so freely.

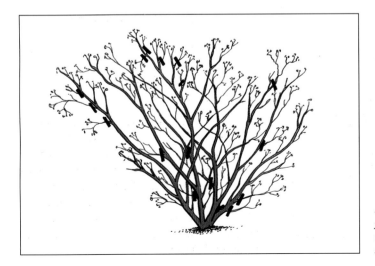

Some shrubs need very little pruning, and only a light trim on an irregular basis is sufficient.

Spring Pruning

Deciduous shrubs which produce flowers on the current season's growth have a tendency to become congested with many small spindly shoots. This leads to a gradual deterioration in both the quantity and quality of the flowers. These shrubs will generally produce vigorous shoots carrying flowers in summer or early autumn if they are pruned in the spring. Shortening the overall length of the flower stems in autumn will reduce the risk of root damage caused by wind rock.

Most large shrubs, such as deciduous *Ceanothus*, develop a woody framework, and in the first season after planting, the main stems of less vigorous shrubs should be lightly pruned. In the second spring, the previous year's growth is reduced by half its length. In subsequent years, hard pruning to leave only two or three pairs of buds from the previous season's growth is recommended, and this pruning should be carried out in late winter or early spring.

By pruning the framework branches to varying heights, flower production at all levels along these branches will be encouraged. Cut out some of the oldest wood as part of the annual pruning operation on mature specimens, to prevent branch overcrowding. Shrubs which flower in late winter or early spring on wood produced in the previous season, such as *Prunus triloba*, are best pruned hard in spring after flowering. The main stems are reduced by about half in the first spring after planting, to form a basal framework. In subsequent years, cut back all growth to two to three buds of the framework stems, immediately after flowering.

Sub-shrubs, such as *Perovskia*, form a woody base which allows them to be pruned back hard to 15–30cm (6–12in) high stubs annually in spring, leaving one or two buds.

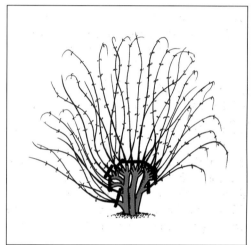

Spring pruning of Buddleja davidii *and* Perovskia.

Shrubs Pruned in Summer after Flowering

Many of the deciduous shrubs which flower in spring or early summer carry their flowers on wood produced in the previous growing season, as with *Chaenomeles* and *Forsythias*, for example. Other shrubs in this group such as *Deutzia*, *Philadelphus* and *Weigela* produce short side-shoots on last year's wood, which will carry the current season's flowers.

Prune in the spring by reducing the overall length of the shoots.

Many shrubs in this group have a natural tendency to develop large amounts of dense twiggy growth, often becoming top-heavy, with poor flower production in terms of both quantity and quality. Without regular pruning to encourage the development of vigorous, young growths from close to ground level, their ornamental value diminishes rapidly.

The ideal time for pruning Forsythia *is just as the flowers begin to wither and die.*

ROOT PRUNING

Root pruning is sometimes used as a means of controlling the vigour of shrubs, or to make them produce more flowers. In the late winter or early spring, dig a trench around the plant you wish to root prune, between 30–60cm (1–2ft) deep with a circumference just wider than the spread of the shrub's canopy of branches. Cut through the thick, woody roots with a pruning saw or loppers, but leave the fibrous roots unpruned.

With old, established shrubs, divide the process into three sections, and prune a third of the root system each year. At this stage it may be that complete removal of the shrub is the best course of action.

Shrubs in this group should be pruned immediately after planting. Cut out all weak or damaged growth and trim back the main shoots to a healthy bud or pair of buds, to encourage the development of a strong new shoots. Prune again immediately after flowering, by cutting back all flower-bearing shoots to a strong bud or pair of buds and remove any thin, weak shoots, to keep a well-balanced shape.

As plants mature, a more drastic pruning regime is usually required to encourage the growth of new replacement shoots. After the third year, this is achieved by cutting out up to 20 per cent of the oldest stems each year to within 5–8cm (2–3in) of the ground. Great care must be taken, since harsh pruning on young shrubs in this group, e.g. *Forsythias*, may result in an unmanageable plant with an irregular shape.

Other shrubs in this group, especially when grown as free-standing shrubs, rather than as wall shrubs, require very little pruning. *Chaenomeles*, for example, has a naturally twiggy habit, with numerous crossing branches, and mature specimens need little pruning. Spur pruning will, however, encourage heavier flowering, so shorten the

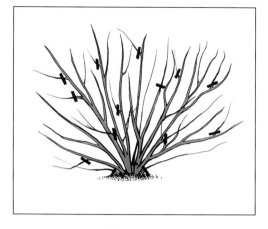

Summer pruning of Weigela.

Prune Kerria *immediately after flowering.*

spurs and side shoots to three to five leaves each in midsummer.

Care must be taken when pruning shrubs such as *Syringa* (lilacs) that develop their new growth as they are flowering. The new shoots forming immediately below the flowers are easily damaged when the old flower heads are removed, which will reduce the number of flowers next year.

A few shrubs such as *Kerria japonica*, which are grown for their flowers, produce

Kerria, *if left unpruned, forms a congested mass of suckering growth.*

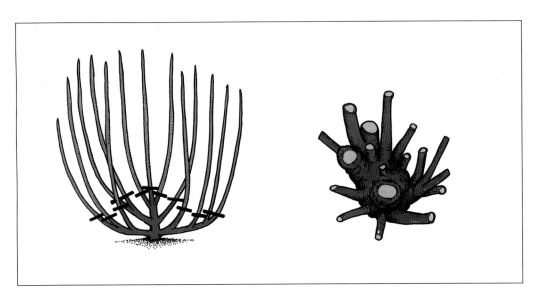

Prune Corus *in late-winter or early spring to produce plenty of attractive coloured stems.*

blooms on wood of the previous year but make most of their new growth from ground level. These shrubs spread by suckers and are pruned as soon as the flowers have faded, by cutting out much of the old, flower-bearing growth, close to soil level.

Shrubs grown for the ornamental value of their stems, such as *Cornus alba*, or leaves such as *Sambucus racemosa* and 'Plumosa Aurea' (Golden elder), require severe spring pruning annually, or biennially in the case of *Cornus alba* 'Sibirica' (Red dogwood), which is much less vigorous.

The method of hard pruning used on these shrubs is essentially a modification of traditional methods of managing trees and shrubs to give a constant and renewable supply of shoots. Most of these trees and shrubs that are cut back regularly to near ground level would normally flower on shoots formed the previous season, but with this technique, the flowers are sacrificed.

With shrubs coppiced for their brightly coloured foliage, much larger leaves are usually produced. Vigorous shrubs such as *Salix alba* 'Chermesina' (Willow) are hard pruned to within about 5–8cm (2–3in) of ground level, to ensure a regular display of highly attractive, brightly coloured young shoots, which are more striking in the winter. Alternatively, the height to which these stems are cut back can be varied to avoid a rigid, uniform effect.

A variation on the coppicing theme is known as pollarding. This gives the same effect, but on the top of a leg or stem, anything up to 2m (6ft) above ground level.

Formative pruning in the first year after planting is used to establish the framework. Start before growth commences in spring, and cut back a young plant to form a standard with a single stem of 30–90cm (1–3ft). During the plant's first growing season, restrict the number of shoots growing from below the cut to only four or five, rubbing out all others and any that develop low down on the main stem. Continue this process for the next year or two; this will allow the main stem to thicken so that it will be able to support heavier top-growth.

In the spring of the second and subsequent years, reduce the previous season's growths to above a bud within 5–8cm (2–3in) of the framework. If a larger specimen is needed, prune only half or one third of the stems.

EVERGREEN SHRUBS

Generally speaking, evergreen shrubs need very little formative pruning indeed, with excessive growth resulting in a lop-sided, unbalanced shape to the plant. Plants in this group should be lightly pruned in mid-spring, soon after they have been planted.

The appropriate pruning method for most evergreen shrubs will depend upon the ultimate size of the plants when they reach maturity. Certain factors will not vary regardless of size; always prune out all dead and diseased wood back to a point where the shrub has started to re-grow, or where live tissue can be seen. If there are any overcrowded or rubbing shoots, these can be

A badly pruned Prunus laurocerasus *demonstrating a lack of understanding of the shrub's growth habit.*

thinned out, and any plants showing signs of die-back following a hard winter, should be cut back to live growth after the risk of a hard frost has passed.

Large Shrubs

These are plants of more than 3m (10ft) tall, e.g. large Rhododendrons, *Prunus laurocerasus* (laurels) and other tall evergreens. They need very little regular pruning, but may require some formative pruning as young plants to create a well-shaped, balanced framework.

This should be carried out on young plants in mid-spring or soon after flowering. Cut out any weak and crossing branches. The objective is to create an open-centred plant with evenly spaced branches.

In subsequent years, routine pruning is generally only necessary to remove dead, damaged, and diseased wood, cut out thin straggly growths, and to shape the plant in order to restrict overall size. To maintain the overall balance and shape of the plant, reduce the length of any strong over-vigorous shoots.

Medium-Sized Evergreen Shrubs

These are plants of up to 3m (10ft) tall, e.g. *Berberis × stenophylla, Camellias, Escallonia,* and many of the large-

---

FORMATIVE PRUNING OF LARGE

First Year
Spring
Prune in mid-spring, cut out any weak and crossing branches, to create an open centred plant with evenly spaced branches.

Summer
With shrubs that flower from midsummer onwards, cut out the old dead flower-heads in late summer or early autumn.

ROUTINE PRUNING OF LARGE SHRUBS

Spring
Cut out any dead, damaged, and diseased wood, remove thin, straggly shoots, and reduce the length of any strong, vigorous shoots affecting the overall balance of the plant to restrict overall size.

Summer
With shrubs that flower from midsummer onwards, cut out old flowering stems in late summer or early autumn.

Frost-damaged tip-growth on a broad-leaved evergreen (in this case,
Choisya ternata*).*

leaved   Rhododendron
hybrids.

In   mid-spring,   just
before   the   new   growth
starts, reduce the length of
any strong, vigorous shoots
which may affect the overall balance and shape of
the plant. In addition, cut
out any weak shoots and
those which are crossing
or rubbing together. In
subsequent years, pruning
is usually only necessary
to cut out thin, straggly
shoots, and either to shape
the plant or to restrict
its overall size, depending
upon the individual situation of the plant within the
garden.

FORMATIVE PRUNING OF MEDIUM-SIZED EVERGREEN SHRUBS

First Year

Spring
Cut back any excessively
vigorous shoots by two-
thirds, and remove any
thin, spindly shoots to
encourage new growth
from the base of the
plant.

Remove any flowers to
encourage the develop-
ment of a strong bushy
plant.

Second Year

Spring
Cut out any weak or crossing shoots which are rubbing together. Reduce in length any strong, vigorous shoots affecting the
overall shape of the plant.

ROUTINE PRUNING OF MEDIUM-SIZED EVERGREEN SHRUBS

Spring
In subsequent years, cut out thin, straggly shoots, and shape the plant to
restrict overall size, and fill its allotted
space within the garden.

For winter or spring-flowering
shrubs, such as *Viburnum tinus*, prune
immediately after flowering.

Summer
With shrubs which flower from midsummer onwards, prune by cutting out
old flowering stems in late summer or
early autumn.

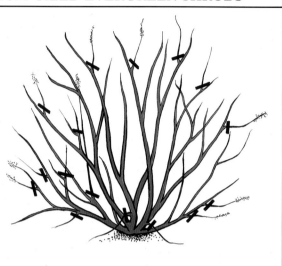

Those shrubs which are winter or spring-
flowering, such as *Berberis darwinii* and
Viburnum tinus, should be pruned immediately after flowering. Plants such as *Photinia
× fraserii* and *Pieris japonica* cultivars, are
grown for their attractive, brightly coloured
new shoots. They should be trimmed to
keep their shape in the summer, after these
coloured shoots turn green.

Others, such as *Escallonia*, *Olearia ×
macrodonta* and *Osmanthus heterophyllus*,
which flower from midsummer onwards,
are pruned in mid-spring by removing the
older wood when the new growth starts, or
in late summer by cutting out the old stems
bearing the spent flowers.

Small Evergreen Shrubs

Small evergreen shrubs which are 1 metre
(or yard) or less can be divided into two
basic groups, with each of these groups
requiring different pruning techniques.

Group One
This group includes a number of shrubs
which are relatively short-lived (generally

about ten years or so) and if left unpruned
for a number of years should be removed
and replaced; although they will flower
abundantly, if they are trimmed annually.
Examples are shrubs such as: *Lavandula*
(lavender), *Santolina chamaecyparissus* (cot-
ton lavender), *Calluna*, *Daboecia*, and *Erica*,
(most heathers but not the tall tree heaths).

The best time to prune the plants in this
category is mid- to late spring, particularly
in cold areas where the risk of die-back
caused by severe frost and wind chill can be
very real. Always start by cutting out any
weak growth and all old shoots which have
flowered. The aim of this type of pruning is
to encourage new growth from the centre of
the plant, and as close to the base as possible. In subsequent years, remove the old
flower heads and completely cut out any
dead, diseased, or damaged shoots.

Group Two
This group includes the prostrate *Cotoneasters* and *Hebes* (Veronicas) as well as most
low-growing shrubs of slow or moderately
vigorous growth rate. These shrubs require
little or no regular pruning, and even dead-

Rhododendron, starting to grow after severe remedial pruning.

If left unpruned, lavender will become bare and open in the centre (below).

PRUNING SMALL SHRUBS – GROUP ONE

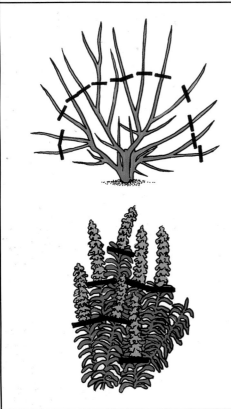

Formative Pruning

Spring
Cut back all shoots by two-thirds to encourage new growth from the base of the shoots in the middle of the plant.

Routine Pruning

Spring
Prune out any dead, diseased, or damaged shoots, all thin weak growths, and remove old flowering shoots, as this encourages new growth from the centre of the plant.

In subsequent years, completely remove any dead, diseased, or damaged shoots and remove the old flower-heads.

PRUNING SMALL SHRUBS – GROUP TWO

Formative Pruning

Spring
Cut back all shoots by two-thirds, and remove any flowers to encourage new growth from the base of the plant.

Routine Pruning

Spring
Prune out any dead, diseased, or damaged shoots, and all thin, weak growths to promote new growth from the centre of the plant.

In subsequent years, little or no regular pruning is required. Many of the *Cotoneasters* are grown for their attractive berries so dead-heading is not necessary. Cut out any dead, diseased, or damaged shoots, in the spring.

heading is not necessary as many *Cotoneasters* are grown for their attractive berries produced in the autumn. The main purpose of pruning the plants in this group is to reduce the risk of pests and diseases, by removing dead, damaged, or diseased shoots in mid-spring.

RENOVATION PRUNING

The first question to consider is whether or not the plants in question are

A shrub border after remedial pruning.

If the shrub is too large for its allotted space, no amount of pruning will be sufficient (right).

worth trying to save. One course of action is to dig them up and start again with young shrubs. This may certainly be the best method in some circumstances, but will not always be necessary, as many shrubs have remarkable powers of recovery and with drastic pruning can be rejuvenated in a relatively short period of time.

Old, neglected, or straggly shrubs often respond to severe pruning and this can be used to renovate plants rather than discard them. Shrubs that respond well

REMEDIAL PRUNING

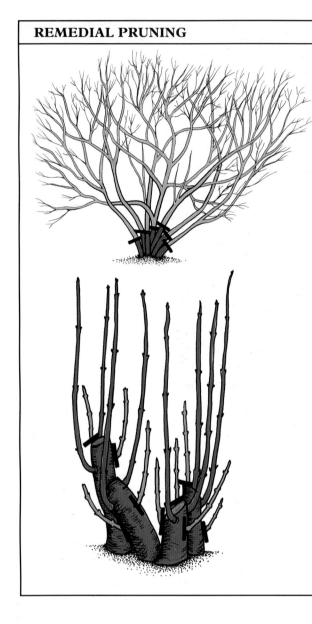

First Year

Winter/Spring
Prune out all the weak stems to ground level, to promote new growth from the base of the plant.

Cut back the main stems to within 30cm (1ft) of the base.

Second Year

Winter/Spring
During the following winter, cut back the resultant new shoots to their point of origin, leaving only two or three of the strongest and best-placed shoots on each stump to start the new framework of the plant.

Any stumps which have not produced worthwhile growths after the first year should be removed at ground level.

Third and Subsequent Years

In the third and subsequent years the pruning technique appropriate to the shrub concerned should be employed, as part of a normal growing cycle.

Further growths will appear from the stumps for a year or two after rejuvenation pruning. Cut out these entirely as they appear, unless they are suitably placed to fill gaps in the framework.

usually produce young growth from the base, but it is pointless trying this method with shrubs which are badly diseased. It is also worth remembering that not all shrubs will take kindly to this treatment e.g. *Cytisus* (broom) will die rather than produce new growths when pruned in this way.

In spite of the gardener's best intentions many vigorous shrubs, such as *Philadelphus*

(Mock orange), lilacs and the hardy hybrid Rhododendrons either become too large for their positions or become overgrown through neglect. Sometimes you may move to a new house to find the garden full of unpruned shrubs which appear beyond redemption.

The faint-hearted or cautious may feel that this rejuvenation process is too drastic. If you feel that the plant is in poor health and may

Green (reverted) growth emerging on Elaeagnus pungens *'Maculata'.*

PHASED REMEDIAL PRUNING

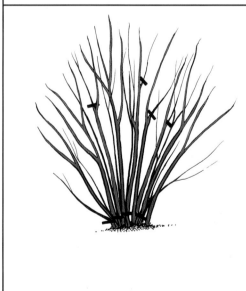

First Year

Winter/Spring

Prune out half of the existing stems to within 5–7.5cm (2–3ins) of ground level, to promote new growth from the base of the plant.

Cut out any crossing shoots which are rubbing together. Reduce in length any strong vigorous shoots affecting the overall shape of the plant.

Cut back any remaining older shoots by half to new healthy growth, and remove any weak spindly growth.

Second Year

Winter/Spring

Cut back the remaining old, main stems.

Any stumps which have not produced worthwhile growths after the first year should be removed at ground level.

Remove all flowering wood immediately after flowering.

SHRUB PRUNING (SEASONAL GUIDE)

SUBJECT	EVERGREEN/ DECIDUOUS	PRUNING TIME	RESPONSE TO RENOVATION
Abelia × *grandiflora*	D	1	√
Acer palmatum cvs	D	0	X
Aucuba japonica cvs	E	0	√
Berberis darwinii	E	1	√
Berberis × *stenophylla*	E	1	√
Berberis thunbergii cvs	D	1	√
Buddleja alternifolia	D	2	√
Buddleja davidii cvs	D	1	√
Buxus sempervirens	E	1	√
Callicarpa bodinieri	D	1	√
Calluna vulgaris cvs	E	1	√
Camellia cvs	E	0	√
Caryopteris × *clandonensis*	D	1	√
Ceratostigma willmottianum	D	1	√
Chaenomeles speciosa cvs	D	1–2	√
Chaenomeles × *superba* cvs	D	1–2	√
Choisya ternata cvs	E	0	√
Cistus × *corbariensis*	E	0	√
Cornus alba cvs	D	1	√
Corylus avellana cvs	D	1	√
Cotinus coggygria cvs	D	0	√
Cotoneaster congestus	E	0	√
Cotoneaster conspicuous cvs	E	0	√
Cotoneaster dammerii	E	0	√
Cotoneaster franchetii	E	0	√
Cotoneaster horizontalis	D	0	√
Cotoneaster microphyllus	E	0	√
Cotoneaster 'Rothchildianus'	E	0	√
Cytisus × *praecox*	D	0	X
Daphne mezereum	D	1	√
Deutzia × hybrida 'Mont Rose'	D	2	√
Elaeagnus × *ebbingei*	E	0	√
Elaeagnus pungens cvs	E	0	√
Erica herbacea cvs	E	1	√
Erica cinerea cvs	E	1–2	√
Escallonia cvs	E	3	√
Euonymus fortunei cvs	E	0	√
Euonymus japonicus cvs	E	0	√
Exochorda × *macrantha* cvs	D	1	√
Forsythia × *intermedia* cvs	D	1	√
Fuchsia magellanica cvs	D	1–2	√
Garrya elliptica	E	0	X
Griselinia littoralis	E	1–2	√
Hamamelis × *intermedia* cvs	D	1	X
Hebe 'Autumn Glory'	E	1–2	√
Helianthemum 'Ben More'	E	0	√
Hibiscus syriacus cvs	D	0	√
Hydrangea macrophylla cvs	D	2–3	√
Hypericum 'Hidcote'	E	1	√
Ilex × *altaclarensis* cvs	E	0	√

SHRUB PRUNING (SEASONAL GUIDE)

SUBJECT	EVERGREEN/ DECIDUOUS	PRUNING TIME	RESPONSE TO RENOVATION
Ilex aquifolium cvs	E	0	√
Kerria japonica cvs	D	2–3	√
Kolkwitzia amibilis	D	1–2	√
Lavandula angustifolia cvs	E	1–2	X
Leucothoe fontanesiana cvs	E	1	√
Ligustrum ovalifolium cvs	E	2–3	√
Lonicera nitida cvs	E	2–3	X
Magnolia grandiflora	E	1	√
Magnolia stellata	D	0	X
Mahonia × media cvs	E	1	√
Olearia macrodonta	E	2–3	X
Pernettya mucronata cvs	E	0	√
Philadelphus coronarius	D	2–3	√
Photinia × fraseri cvs	E	0	√
Pieris japonica cvs	E	2	√
Potentilla fruticosa	D	3	√
Prunus laurocerasus cvs	E	0	√
Prunus lusitanica cvs	E	0	√
Prunus triloba	D	2	X
Pyracantha cvs	E	0	√
Rhododendron ponticum	E	2	√
Rhus typhina	D	2	√
Ribes sanguineum cvs	D	2	√
Rosmarinus officinalis	E	2	√
Sambucus nigra cvs	D	1	√
Sambucus racemosa cvs	D	1	√
Santolina chamaecyparissus	E	3	X
Senecio 'Sunshine'	E	3–4	√
Skimmia japonica	E	0	√
Spiraea × arguta	D	2–3	√
Spiraea japonica	D	4–1	√
Symphoricarpus cvs	D	1	√
Syringa vulgaris cvs	D	2–3	√
Viburnum × bodnantense cvs	D	0	√

(1 = spring, 2 = summer)
(3 = autumn, 4 = winter)
(0 = No regular pruning)

not recover from complete stem removal, cut out only a proportion of the main stems. The process can then be completed by removing the remaining old growths after flowering in summer or the following winter.

This two-stage renovation process is suitable for deciduous shrubs such as *Philadelphus*, which naturally renew themselves from basal growths. With evergreens, it is preferable to deal with the whole plant to avoid the uneven growth which occurs when renovation is carried out over two seasons. Not all shrubs will respond to this treatment, but the percentage which do recover is high, and within three or four years, the shrub should be flowering well once again.

CHAPTER 5

Hedges

A large number of both deciduous and evergreen trees and shrubs will respond to regular clipping by producing an even covering of dense, compact growth useful for garden hedges and windbreaks. The formation of this closely knit dense growth makes these plants ideal for providing shelter for other plants. They can also provide a living barrier for security, or for noise reduction, or form an ornamental feature in their own right.

Hedge clipping is only a different type pruning, carried out in a certain way to achieve a particular purpose and the same general principles apply as with other forms of pruning.

Purple beech makes a perfect screen in this urban setting.

Fuchsia makes an attractive informal hedge (above).

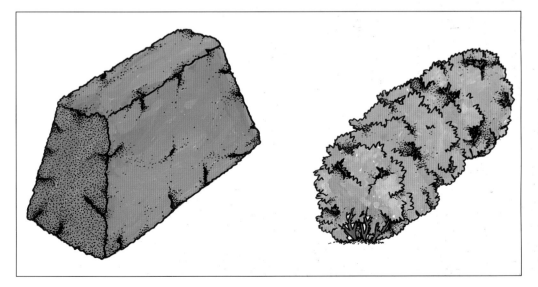

Hedges can be either: formal (left) *or informal* (right). *Informal hedges are pruned less frequently and allowed to flower.*

HEDGE TYPES

Formal hedges are those which require regular clipping or trimming to restrict growth and maintain their shape. They make excellent living barriers, and provide a perfect backdrop for other ornamental plants in a formal setting.

Informal hedges, on the other hand, are given only the bare minimum of pruning to encourage the individual plants to flower and prevent them from becoming overgrown with straggly, wayward shoots. To some gardeners this type of hedge may look too untidy, but they can be very attractive, and there is far less work involved to achieve the desired effect. Exactly how and when they are pruned depends mainly upon when they flower; but as a general rule, they are best pruned soon after flowering, and it is the flower-bearing branches which are removed.

Those plants which produce fruits, such as hips or berries should not be pruned until the fruits have finished.

Tapestry Hedges

These are hedges which are made up of a mixture of plants such as *Fagus sylvatica* (Beech) alternated with *Taxus baccata* (Yew) or *Ilex* (Holly) This type of hedge provides a range of visual interests as the plants change with the seasons.

Certainly a mixture of deciduous and evergreen species provides a colourful background, but plants with similar growth rates must be chosen or the faster growing plants will become dominant. Here they are mentioned separately as the pruning may vary slightly from hedges which consist of one plant type only. Obviously, with no two plants having exactly the same growth habit and rate, slightly different pruning techniques may have to be used. Plants can be selected for flower or foliage contrasts, or both.

FORMATIVE PRUNING AND TRAINING

Many gardeners are reluctant to prune young hedging plants at all during the first year or two, but this formative pruning is essential to newly planted hedges as it promotes an even distribution of growth at the base as well as the top of the hedge. It is also a good way of ensuring that they do not grow too high too quickly.

Most hedging plants benefit greatly from being cut back to two thirds of their original height immediately after planting. At the same time, any strong, lateral branches can be cut back by about half. This encourages each plant to form a dense bushy habit, and cutting down the size of each plant is a very effective way of reducing its wind resistance, which in turn helps the plant to establish much more rapidly.

This process is repeated in the second year to develop a tight framework of growth. Also, by severely pruning the sides and top of the hedge, most of the extension growth forms between the plants, thus forcing them to grow into one another. By doing this, they cease to become a row of individual plants, and start to become a hedge.

The severity of this initial pruning will depend on the kind of hedging plant used, but the main aim is to encourage the hedge to make plenty of bottom growth, otherwise the base may remain relatively bare while the upper part of the hedge is dense. The importance of correct initial training cannot be over-emphasized, as the success of the hedge depends on the treatment given to it during the first two or three years.

The feeding of hedges is often neglected, and annual mulches of well-rotted compost or manure are advisable to maintain vigour. This will go towards compensating for the fact that much of the plant's food production capacity is lost by clipping and removing the leaves.

FORMATIVE PRUNING

First Year

Winter
Immediately after planting, cut the plants back to between half and two thirds of their original height (deciduous plants will tolerate harder pruning than evergreens).

Summer/Autumn
As the new shoots develop, lightly trim any shoots growing out at right angles to the hedge to keep it bushy and growing upright. Cut out the growing point of any over vigorous plants.

Second Year

Winter
Cut the plants back by one third of the new growth and, shorten any laterals growing out of place.

Spring/Summer
As the new shoots develop, lightly trim any shoots growing out at right angles to the hedge to keep it bushy and growing upright. Cut out the growing point of any over vigorous plants.

Third Year

Spring and Autumn
As the shoots develop start trimming for shape and thickness as required.

MAINTENANCE PRUNING

The main purpose of clipping is to produce a hedge of the desired height and width which is well furnished with growth over its entire growing surface. If a hedge is pruned and trimmed correctly in the early stages of development, there is no need for it to exceed 75cm (2.5ft) in width (this applies to even the most vigorous species of hedge plants). This is particularly important as the wider the hedge is allowed to become the more difficult it is to trim, especially the top, and the more space it occupies.

The sloping angle of the hedge is called the 'batter', and creating this batter will expose all parts of the hedge to the light and stop parts of it dying out, especially at the base.

Formal hedges should always be narrower at the top than at the base, to make trimming easier. If the hedge is wider at the top than at the base, it is prone to damage by strong winds because the hedge is top heavy and the branches are opened up.

Even more of a problem is caused where the top is flat, as snow settling and accumulating on the top of the hedge can make cause the branches spread or 'splay out', causing considerable damage to the branches. This is a much greater problem with evergreen species as they can collect large quantities of snow and ice in cold winter weather.

When clipping a formal hedge, always plan out the work before you start. This can save time in the long run:

1. Start at the bottom, to establish the ideal width required and then work upwards.

Trim the hedge to encourage a thick, dense habit.

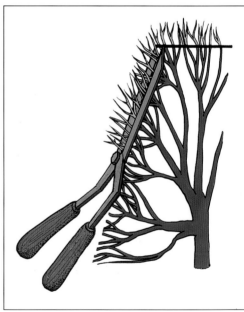

Work systematically, cutting from the base upwards.

This means that the clippings will fall out of the way once they have been cut, making it easier to see where to cut next. Cutting from the top down will often result in clippings accumulating and pulling down branches: when these are cut off, an uneven surface is left. When cutting with shears, always have the point slightly tilted in towards the hedge so that the tapered sides (the batter) can be maintained. If a mechanical hedge trimmer is used, always cut upwards in

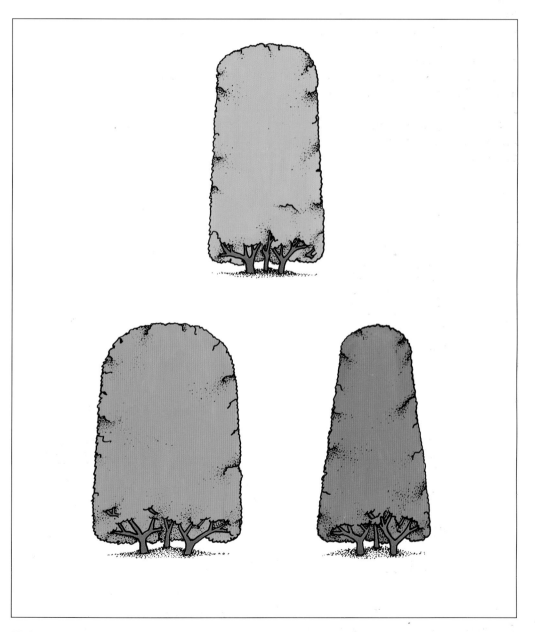

Hedge profiles.

Hedges are ideal for sheltering ornamental plants.

a sweeping arc-like action, and keep the cutting bar parallel to the hedge.

2. To achieve a level hedge-top, use a garden line stretched taut between two posts, at a set height. This ensures the correct level is achieved as the work progresses. Use a string with a vivid colour, as this makes it much easier to follow the line without cutting through it.

3. If a particular hedge profile is required, use a pre-cut template, which will straddle the hedge, and move this across the hedge as you work.

4. With hedges over 2m (6ft) in height, use two stepladders with a standing board in between, and where possible have another person working with you.

5. When the hedge has reached its required height, cut the top down to 30cm (1ft) below this height. The top of the hedge will then grow bushy and strong as it responds to pruning. Also, you will not see any woody stumps from the pruning cuts, or sections of bare stem, as they will be hidden by the new growth.

Normally, hand or electric shears will be used for clipping hedges. With broadleaved evergreens such as *Prunus laurocerasus* (Common laurel) secateurs should be used, as pruning with shears will mutilate many larger leaves and spoil the overall effect of the hedge until new growth has developed.

Leaves which are cut in half develop a brown line where the cells have been damaged and these 'half-leaves' slowly turn yellow and die. During this process, they are very prone to invasion by pests and diseases.

Where the hedge is too long for trimming with secateurs, use shears for the main cut and follow this by using secateurs to trim any badly damaged, unsightly foliage.

RENOVATION (REMEDIAL PRUNING)

It is inevitable that over a period of time, a hedge may become too wide, damaged by weather (or some other cause) or overgrown through neglect. At this point, a difficult decision has to be made; whether or not it is preferable to dig out the whole hedge and replace it with young plants and start all over again; or to try and renovate the hedge with very drastic remedial pruning.

There is also the soil to consider, and replanting with the same species can create a host of problems, with the new plants often suffering from 'replant disease' or 'soil sickness'. The symptoms of these are slow, stunted growth, and, in extreme cases, they can result in the death of the newly introduced plants. This is particularly common in members of the family *Rosaceae*, which includes:

Chaenomeles (Quince)
Cotoneaster (Cotoneaster)
Crateagus (Hawthorn)
Prunus (Cherry and Laurel)
Pyrus (Pear)
Rosa (Roses)
Sorbus (Rowan and Mountain ash)

To overcome this particular problem is only really possible by digging out a trench and replacing all of the original soil; employing a contractor to sterilize the soil

Some conifers start to show old dead foliage if not pruned regularly.

RENOVATION PRUNING

First Year

Spring
Cut back the growth on one side of the hedge to within 15cm (6in) of the main stems. (Always trim the sheltered side of the hedge first, as it will respond more quickly.) Lightly trim the growth on the other side of the hedge.

Autumn
If regrowth has been rapid, trim the new growth lightly to encourage the shoots to branch and the foliage to thicken.

Second Year

Spring
Cut back the growth hard on the other side of the hedge to within 15cm (6in) of the main stems. Lightly trim the growth on the side of the hedge which was pruned severely in year one.

by fumigating it (both of which are very expensive); or replanting with a totally unrelated species e.g. replacing *Prunus laurocerasus* (Laurel) hedge with one consisting of *Taxus baccata* (Yew).

Quite often, the decision will be made for you, as some species do not respond well to severe pruning. However, some species will respond very favourably to fairly drastic pruning.

The method used can vary, and in the most extreme cases the plant is cut to within 10cm (4in) of the base, in order to stimulate the production of new shoots from soil level. Of course, if this is done, it means that as the hedge re-grows, the process of formative pruning and training will have to be carried out as for a newly planted hedge.

There are a number of problems with taking such drastic action as it has an effect on the surroundings, reducing privacy and exposing the sheltered area by removing the remaining shelter. A more measured approach is to cut back one side of the hedge to the main stems, for the total height and length of the hedge (this is important to get even growth over the newly pruned surface). This procedure can be repeated on the other side of the hedge the following year, or for a very old hedge two years later, which will allow maximum recovery time.

With broad-leaved evergreens such as *Pyracantha* and *Rhododendron ponticum*, this pruning should be carried out in late spring. Deciduous species should be treated in late winter or early spring. For both types of plant, the timing is important, as they will put on a massive surge of growth at this time of year, which will reduce the recovery time. Most conifers do *not* have the capacity to generate new growth from old wood and are not suited to renovation pruning.

For this process to be successful, it is most important to provide ample feeding and watering to promote rapid growth. If possible, start by mulching the plants in the season before renovation pruning starts, and again after cutting back to encourage healthy new growth.

For the first year, it is also important to examine the cut surfaces regularly to make sure that no invasive fungal diseases such as *Nectria cinnabarina* (Coral Spot) have entered through any of the pruning cuts. Any infected material should be removed and burned immediately.

Hedges provide the perfect foil for other plants.

SUITABLE HEDGING PLANTS

Formal Hedges (clipped)

SUBJECT	EVERGREEN/ DECIDUOUS	BEST HEIGHT	CLIPPING TIMES	RESPONSE TO RENOVATION
Berberis thunbergii (Barberry)	D	0.6–1.2m	1 × in summer	√
Buxus sempervirens (Box)	E	0.3–0.6m	3 × but not in winter	√
Carpinus betulus (Hornbeam)	D	1.5–6.0m	1 × late summer	√
Chamaecyparis lawsoniana (Lawson's cypress)	E	1.2–2.5+m	2 × late spring and early autumn	X
Crataegus monogyna (Hawthorn)	D	1.5–3.0m	2 × summer and autumn	√
× *Cupressocyparis Leylandii* (Leyland Cypress)	E	2.0–6.0m	3 × but not in winter	X
Elaeagnus × *ebbingei* (Elaeagnus)	E	1.5–3.0m	1 × mid- to late summer	√
Escallonia (Escallonia)	E	1.2–2.5m	1 × immediately after flowering	√
Fagus sylvatica (Beech)	D	1.5–6.0m	1 × late summer	√
Griselinia littoralis (Broadleaf)	E	1.2–3.0m	2 × late spring, late summer	X
Ilex aquifolium (Holly)	E	2.0–4.0m	1 × late summer	√
Lavandula (Lavender)	E	0.5–1.0m	2 × in spring and after flowering	X
Ligustrum (Privet)	E	1.5–3.0m	3 × but not in winter	X
Lonicera nitida (Lonicera)	E	0.9–1.2m	3 × but not in winter	X
Prunus laurocerasus (Laurel)	E	1.2–3.0m	1 × mid- to late summer	√
Pyracantha (Firethorn)	E	2.0–3.0m	2 × after flowering and again in autumn but avoid berries	X

SUITABLE HEDGING PLANTS (continued)

SUBJECT	EVERGREEN/ DECIDUOUS	BEST HEIGHT	CLIPPING TIMES	RESPONSE TO RENOVATION
Taxus baccata (Yew)	E	1.2–6.0m	2 × summer and autumn	X
Thuja plicata (Western Red Cedar)	E	1.5–4.0m	2 × late spring and early autumn	X

Informal Hedges (unclipped)

SUBJECT	EVERGREEN/ DECIDUOUS	BEST HEIGHT	CLIPPING TIMES	RESPONSE TO RENOVATION
Berberis darwinii (Barberry)	E	1.5–2.5m	1 × after flowering	√
Berberis thunbergii (Barberry)	D	0.6–1.2m	1 × after flowering	√
Cotoneaster lacteus (Cotoneaster)	E	1.5–2.2m	1 × after fruiting	√
Crataegus monogyna (Hawthorn)	D	.5–3.0m	1 × winter	√
Escallonia (Escallonia)	E	1.2–2.5m	1 × immediately after flowering	√
Forsythia × intermedia (Forsythia)	D	1.5–2.5m	1 × after flowering	√
Fuchsia magellanica	D	0.9–1.5m	1 × in spring to remove old stems	√
Garrya elliptica (Tassel bush)	E	1.5–2.2m	1 × immediately after flowering	X
Ilex aquifolium (Holly)	E	2.0–4.0m	1 × late summer	√
Lavandula (Lavender)	E	0.5–1.0m	2 × in spring and after flowering	X
Pyracantha (Firethorn)	E	2.0–3.0m	2 × after flowering and again in autumn but avoid berries	X
Rosa rugosa (Rose)	D	1.0–1.5m	1 × spring remove oldest shoots	√
Viburnum tinus	E	1.0–2.4m	1 × after flowering	X

CHAPTER 6

Vines

Anyone who has travelled through Europe and other regions of the world where grapes are grown will soon realise that there are many training and pruning methods which are adopted for viticulture.

PRUNING AND TRAINING

The various methods of pruning fall into two basic categories:

1. spur pruning
2. renewal pruning

The usual training method for dessert grapes is to develop a cordon on which permanent fruiting spurs are formed. This can be either single or double stemmed. Both methods are ideal for producing high-quality fruits.

Vines produce fruit on the current season's growth, which means that spring and summer pruning is geared towards restricting the new growth from the side shoots and allowing only one bunch of grapes to develop from each spur. The same pruning process also reduces the foliage canopy enough to aid the ripening of the fruit. This is particularly important during dull weather conditions.

Formative Training and Pruning

After planting, while the vine is dormant, shorten the stem to a strong bud no more than a few inches above the ground. In summer, train one leading shoot onto a vertical

First Year

Winter
Cut the one-year-old vine back to two buds above soil level.

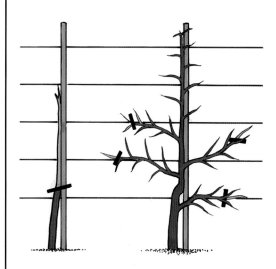

Summer
As the new shoots develop, allow the strongest to grow and tie it to a cane to keep it growing upright. Cut out the growing point of the other shoots when they reach five or six leaves. Any side shoots which develop from these are cut back to a single leaf.

bamboo cane and pinch or cut back the laterals to five or six leaves. Shorten all the sub-laterals to one leaf. Remove any shoots which develop from the base.

During the second winter, cut back the leader to well-ripened wood two thirds of the way down the new growth. The laterals should be cut back to one bud at the same time.

In the second summer, tie in the leading shoot as it extends. Prune side shoots to five

FORMATIVE PRUNING – SINGLE CORDON

Second Year

Winter

Soon after leaf fall, cut the main stem back by two thirds of the new growth and, shorten any laterals to a single bud.

Spring/Summer

The apical (top) bud will grow the fastest and form the new stem. Cut out the growing point of the lateral shoots when they reach five or six leaves. Any side shoots which develop from these are cut back to a single leaf. Remove any flower trusses which form.

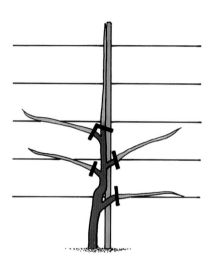

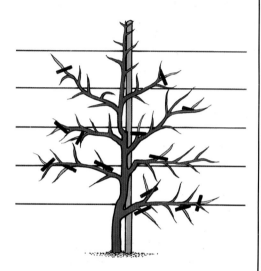

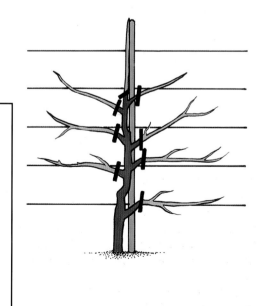

Third Year

Winter

Soon after leaf fall cut this year's extension growth back by two thirds and reduce the laterals back to one strong bud.

Spring/Summer

As the shoots develop from each spur, remove all but two shoots; one will form the main lateral, one is kept in reserve.

or six leaves and sub-laterals to one leaf as for the first summer. Remove any flower trusses; do not allow the vine to fruit until the third year.

In the third winter, shorten the leading shoot by two thirds of its new growth and cut back all the laterals to one strong bud to create spurs which will bear fruiting shoots.

SINGLE CORDON

Formative Pruning

A single cordon plant will take three years to establish a suitable fruit-bearing framework before the regular cropping cycle begins. Start soon after planting, while the vine is still dormant, by cutting the main stem down to a few inches above the ground, leaving at least two strong buds.

During the summer, train one bud onto a vertical bamboo cane, so that it can form the leading shoot (this leading shoot will often grow 1.5–2.0m (5–6ft) in this first year). Over the same period, cut any developing laterals back to five or six leaves. These laterals usually respond by forming branches of their own (called sub-laterals) and these should be cut back to one leaf. Any shoots which develop from the base should be removed as soon as they emerge.

In the second winter, cut back the main shoot by about two-thirds of the new growth, making sure to cut back into brown, well-ripened wood. At the same time, prune any laterals back to a single bud. In the second summer after planting, as it extends, tie the leading shoot onto the vertical bamboo cane. As they develop, cut back the laterals and sub-laterals in exactly the same way as for the previous summer. In order to prevent the vine producing fruit for at least another year, remove any flower trusses which have started to emerge.

During the third winter, prune back the leading shoot, removing about two thirds of

the extension growth made in the previous summer. Cut back all the laterals to one strong bud, so that these become spurs which will, in turn, produce fruiting shoots.

Routine Pruning of Established Plants

Once a fruiting framework has been created, the pruning is very much routine. As the new growth emerges in the spring, allow each spur to produce two shoots. Let the strongest shoot on each spur grow and pinch back the weaker one to two leaves.

Fruiting spurs on an established vine stem.

Also pinch out any other shoots as soon as they start to grow.

This strongest shoot will provide the grapes; keep the weaker shoot as a reserve in case the fruiting shoot becomes damaged or breaks. When the flower trusses develop in the summer, only keep the best, restrict them to one truss on each lateral, and remove the rest. The laterals should be stopped at two leaves beyond each selected flower truss. Any laterals which are not bearing flowers are cut back to five leaves, and sub-laterals to a single leaf.

Every winter, when the leader reaches the top of its support system, prune it back to two buds, and cut the lateral shoots back to a pair of buds. The top half of the leader should be untied from its supports now and carefully bent over until it is lying almost horizontally for a few weeks. This promotes a distribution of plant hormones, which in turn encourage the even development of shoots along the length of the stem in the following spring. Later, the leader can be re-tied vertically before the spring growth starts.

The fruiting spurs should be about 30cm (12in) apart, but during later years some of the spur systems may become overcrowded. It might then be necessary

ROUTINE PRUNING OF ESTABLISHED PLANTS

Spring/Summer
Each fruit-bearing lateral is stopped at a pair of leaves just beyond the first bunch of grapes, and any side growths pinched back to a single leaf. Any lateral shoots not fruiting are cut back to five buds and any weak flower trusses are pinched out.

Winter
Cut back the laterals to two strong buds, and reduce the new growth on the leader to two buds. Tie the top half of the main stem into a horizontal position.

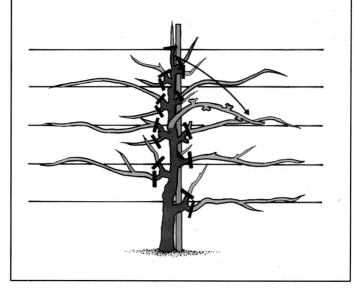

either to remove part of the system with a pruning saw or even to remove some of the spurs completely.

DOUBLE CORDON

Formative Pruning

A double cordon is created by training two shoots horizontally in the first summer, then pruning each shoot back to 60cm (2ft) in length during the winter.

The following spring, train the extension growths vertically to form two arms, each being pruned in exactly the same way as a single cordon.

This process can be repeated again to produce a multiple cordon, so that in the first summer and winter the two shoots are trained, in an identical way for those on the double cordon. In the second spring, continue to train out the two lateral extension growths horizontally, and also choose a strong shoot every 60cm (2ft) to train upright in order to form the number of arms required. There is no limit to the number of upright arms a plant can support and, once established, prune each arm as a single cordon.

Renewal Pruning

There are alternative pruning methods for cultivars which will not produce enough fruit-bearing shoots from the basal buds left by spur pruning. In such cases, longer lengths of ripened wood, or canes, are retained when winter pruning the buds from which fruit-bearing shoots will be produced. Other canes are cut back to three or four buds to produce strong new growths to replace the old fruiting canes the following winter; repeat this process each year.

There are variations on the renewal system used to train dessert grapes, but for wine grapes the Guyot system is the most widely used. This is a system which involves the

THE DOUBLE GUYOT SYSTEM

First Year

Winter
Cut the one-year-old vine back to two buds above soil level.

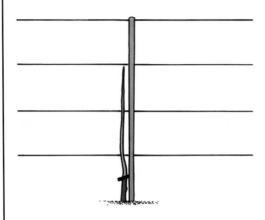

Summer
As the new shoots develop, allow the strongest to grow, tie it to a cane to keep it growing upright.

Cut out the growing point of the other shoots when they reach five or six leaves. Any shoots which compete with the leader are cut back to a single leaf.

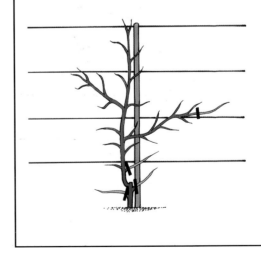

THE DOUBLE GUYOT SYSTEM

Second Year

Winter
Soon after leaf-fall, cut the main stem back to just below the bottom wire, leaving three strong buds.

Third Year

Winter
Soon after leaf-fall, bend down the two outer shoots into a horizontal position and cut them back to 60cm (2ft). Prune the remaining central shoot to three or four strong buds.

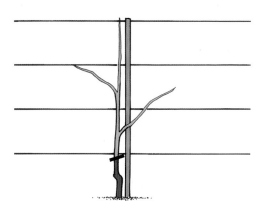

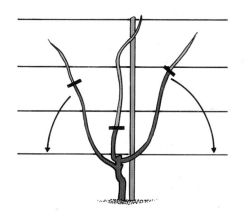

Spring/Summer
Allow three strong shoots to develop, tie them loosely and cut out any other shoots. Remove any flower trusses which form.

Spring/Summer
As the shoots develop along the horizontal stems they are trained vertically up the support wires.

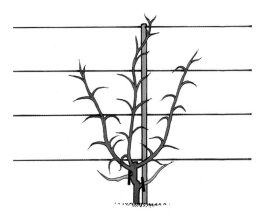

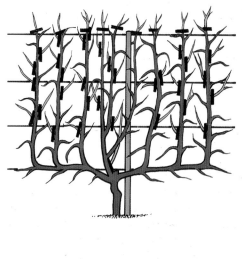

pruning and training of shoots to create horizontal rods from which fruiting shoots are trained vertically. This training has to be done each year, but has the advantage of producing a large quantity of grapes in a confined space.

The Double Guyot System

The double Guyot system (*see* previous page) has a multiple effect whereby two rods from each plant are trained horizontally.

During the first winter, the vine is cut back to two strong buds above ground level. In the first summer, let one shoot develop and tie it to a vertical cane or wire, remove other low shoots, cutting back any lateral shoots to five leaves.

The following winter, cut back the main stem to just below the bottom wire but make sure that at least three strong buds remain. Let three strong shoots develop the next summer and tie them in vertically, removing any low shoots.

In the third winter, tie down the two outer shoots to the bottom wire, one on either side. Tip prune these to eight or ten buds; these will produce fruiting shoots the following summer. The third central shoot is cut back to three or four buds, which will produce replacement shoots, to repeat the whole process the following year.

During the third summer, select three of the best central shoots growing from the stem (rod) and tie loosely to a central post or cane; remove any other competing or weaker shoots growing through the centre. Pinch back to one leaf any side shoots which form on the three selected shoots. Train the shoots from the two arms vertically through the support wires. A few bunches of grapes are allowed to develop on these shoots if growth is vigorous. Any shoots which grow above the top support wire are tipped at two leaves above the wire, and any side shoots on the fruiting stems are removed.

The single Guyot system is very similar to the double system, the only real differences being that:

1. two replacement shoots are grown each year
2. only one shoot is trained horizontally and the other one pruned hard to provide replacement stems.

Routine Pruning of Established Plants

For winter pruning of established vines, cut out all old, fruited wood leaving only three replacement shoots. Tie two of these shoots down, one on either side of the centre and tip prune as for the third winter. Prune the third shoot to three strong buds. Routine summer pruning and training of replacement shoots is as for the third summer. Cut out any overcrowded shoots obscuring the fruits, and completely remove any leaves shading the grapes about six weeks before they are expected to ripen.

VINES FOR OUTDOOR CULTIVATION

These fall into two main groups:

1. Those suitable for dessert.

   Brant (B)
   Muscat Bleu (B)
   New York Muscat (W)
   Noir Hatif de Marseilles (B)
   Perle de Czaba (W)
   Tereshkova (B)

2. Those suitable for wine:

   Huxelrebe (W)
   Siegerrebe (G)
   Bacchus (W)
   Muller Thurgau (W)
   Pinot Noir (B)

(B) = Black fruit; (G) = Golden fruit
(W) = White fruit

ROUTINE PRUNING OF ESTABLISHED PLANTS

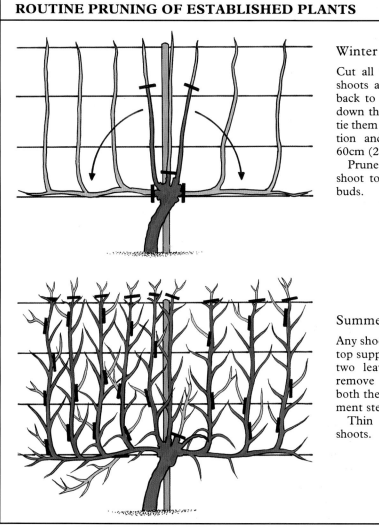

Winter

Cut all the old, fruit-bearing shoots and horizontal laterals back to the main stem, bend down the replacement shoots, tie them into a horizontal position and cut them back to 60cm (2ft).

Prune the remaining central shoot to three or four strong buds.

Summer

Any shoots growing above the top support wire are tipped at two leaves above the wire, remove any side shoots on both the fruiting and replacement stems.

Thin out overcrowded shoots.

GROWING VINES INDOORS

In this particular context, 'indoors' is usually either a greenhouse (often a lean-to type), or, more commonly, a conservatory. It is unusual for a greenhouse to be dedicated purely to viticulture, and for this reason, vines very rarely get ideal growing conditions, simply because they are having to share with other plants. In this situation, it is important to select and grow plants which are compatible with the vine for temperature and humidity requirements. However, it is worth remembering that most vines are quite hardy, although they do need protection to extend the growing season and to protect the fruit while it ripens.

Pruning and Training

The usual method for dessert grapes grown indoors is to grow them up in the roof of the glasshouse. A single stem runs the length of the structure, and fruiting spurs are formed

Outdoor vines immediately after pruning and tying down in winter.

The crops of grapes are produced on the current season's growth.

on lateral branches which are grown (often at right angles) from this main stem.

Much of the pruning of vines is carried out in the spring and summer. As vines produce fruit on the current year's shoots, reducing the crop to one bunch of grapes on each spur greatly improves the size and quality of the fruit. Also, this summer pruning restricts extension growth and reduces leaf cover, allowing more sun to get to the fruit and aid the ripening process.

In the winter, all of the laterals are cut back to 3cm (1in). Often at this stage the vine is lowered to the ground in order to encourage even growth along its entire length when the new shoots emerge in the spring.

Never prune established indoor vines between full dormancy and full leaf, as they are very prone to sap bleeding because the root system is more active than the top growth.

Formative Pruning

Immediately after planting, cut the stem back to two buds just above ground level. Ideally this is done between November and January, while the vine is still dormant.

As it grows in the summer, train the leading shoot onto a vertical bamboo cane and pinch or cut back laterals to five or six leaves (about 10cm or 4in). Any developing sub-laterals are stopped at the first leaf, and any shoots coming from the base are removed.

During the second winter, reduce the leader by two thirds of the new growth, cutting into well-ripened wood. In the second summer, tie in the leading shoot as it

New shoots emerging in the spring from the base of an indoor vine.

FORMATIVE PRUNING OF THE INDOOR VINE

First Year

November–January
Cut the one-year-old vine back to two buds above soil level.

April–September
As the new shoots develop, allow the strongest to grow. Pinch out the growing point of the other shoots when they reach 10cm (4in) long. Any side shoots which develop from these are cut back to a single leaf.

Winter
Cut the vine back by two thirds, soon after leaf fall.

Second Year

March–April
The apical (top) bud will grow the fastest and form the new stem. Allow the laterals to form, but remove any which are too close together by pinching them out when they are 3cm (1in) long.

May–September
Stop the laterals when they reach 60cm (2ft) in length.

Winter
Soon after leaf fall cut this year's extension growth back by half and reduce the laterals back to two strong buds.

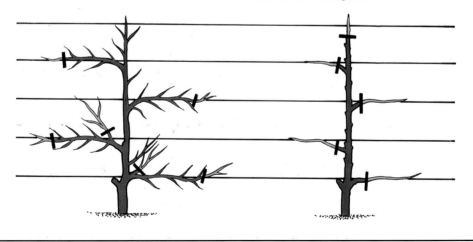

extends. Prune side shoots to five or six leaves and sub-laterals to one leaf as for the first summer. Remove any flower trusses; do not allow the vine to fruit until the third year.

Routine Pruning

The pruning from this stage is now very much routine. Allow the main stem to grow until it reaches the farthest limit of the glasshouse, reducing its growth by summer pruning and cutting the new growth back to a single bud in the winter. All laterals are pinched out or pruned at two leaves beyond a bunch of grapes, with sub-laterals stopped at a single leaf.

The vine is trimmed after harvest, which involves cutting back the laterals by half, and is done to keep the plant tidy. In the winter, cut the laterals back to two buds to form tight spurs.

It is important not to allow the vine to overcrop, particularly the number of grapes on a single bunch, or the result will be large numbers of small grapes, which encourages rotting. In order to prevent this, the grapes are thinned with thin scissors as they begin to swell. Remove the grapes from the centre of the bunch, to allow those remaining to swell unhindered. Great care must be taken not to handle the grapes or they may bruise and start to rot. The thinned bunches of grapes should be wide at the top (the shoulders) and tapering to a point at the base, as this shape encourages even ripening.

ROUTINE PRUNING OF THE INDOOR VINE

Third Year Onwards

April–July
Encourage the leading shoot to grow up into the roof of the house. Continue to train the laterals horizontally at right angles to the main stem and aim for a lateral every 15cm (6in) along the stem.

Each fruit-bearing lateral is stopped at a pair of leaves just beyond the first bunch of grapes, and side growths are pinched back to a single leaf.

Autumn
After harvesting the fruit, cut the laterals back to half their length.

Winter
Cut back the laterals to two strong buds, and remove the end third of the leader.

When pruning, strip away the old loose bark from the stem as this is an ideal site for pests and diseases to gather.

VINES FOR INDOOR CULTIVATION

These fall into three main groups:

Muscats: these have the best flavour, but may be difficult to pollinate and must have heat for the fruit to attain full flavour e.g.

    Canon Hall Muscat (W)
    Fontignan (B & W)
    Madresfield Court (B)
    Muscat of Alexandria (W)

Sweetwater: these are early, quick maturing, do not hang well on the vine but are ideal for growing in an unheated glasshouse e.g.

    Black Hamburgh (B)
    Buckland Sweetwater (W)
    Fosters Seedling (W)
    Lady Hutt (W)

Vinous: these are very late maturing, vigorous grapes that need to hang on the vine in a heated glasshouse for a long period e.g.

    Alicante (B)
    Lady Downes Seedling (B)
    Syrian (W)
    Trebbiano (W)

(B) = Black fruits   (W) = White fruits

CHAPTER 7

Soft Fruit

All of the fruit-bearing plants to which we refer as soft fruit can be divided into either: cane fruits (including blackberries, loganberries and raspberries), or bush fruits (including all of the currants, black, red and white, blueberries and gooseberries). The one exception within this group is the strawberry, which is an herbaceous perennial.

CANE FRUITS

These plants bear their fruit only on one-year-old stems, so that these canes will only ever carry one crop, and over a short period of time, these old fruiting shoots will gradually die. There are one or two exceptions to this rule of thumb; the blackberry cultivar 'Himalaya Giant', has persistent canes which can bear fruit for more than one year. It is, however, normal practice to cut out the old fruiting canes each year, even with these cultivars.

Formative Pruning

Immediately after planting new canes, cut them back to about 23cm (9in) above soil level to encourage strong, vigorous shoots to emerge from the base of the new plant. This

---

FORMATIVE PRUNING
Winter/Spring Cut the new canes back to about 23cm (9in) above the ground.

---

also prevents the newly planted cane from fruiting, which speeds up establishment.

Routine Pruning and Training

One of the main functions of pruning is to ensure an annual supply of new shoots to replace those which have carried the fruit. For this reason, pruning is usually carried out immediately after fruiting and involves cutting down to soil level and removing those stems which carried the fruit. When pruning, it is important to remove any thin, weak, diseased or damaged canes, in order to keep the plants cropping regularly.

With some of the cane fruits such as blackberries and loganberries the main aims of training are:

1. to separate the fruiting canes from the young, newly developing canes, which helps to reduce the spread of pests and diseases
2. to space the fruiting canes to aid ripening and make picking easier
3. to make it easier to prune out the old canes and train in the new ones.

For most gardeners, an open-fan system is used to train the plants, a system which is especially useful where space is limited.

The new shoots which were growing in a central column are spread out so that they are about 30cm (1ft) apart, and are tied in a fan arrangement along the supporting wires. Any weak or damaged shoots are removed as the work progresses. A final check is made in late winter or early spring,

ESTABLISHED BLACKBERRIES, LOGANBERRIES AND HYBRID BERRIES

Spring/Summer
As the new canes start to grow, gather them together and tie loosely between the two wings of the fan.

Summer/Autumn
Immediately after harvest cut down all the old fruiting canes close to ground level. Spread out the new canes and train them along the wire supports, removing any canes which are surplus to requirements.

Leave a space in the centre of the plant for the new canes to be tied when they develop.

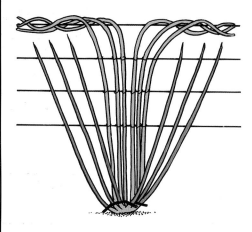

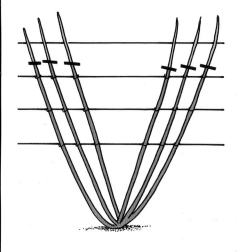

An old dead shoot being removed from a loganberry.

Spring
Prune back the tip of each cane if it shows any signs of frost damage or die-back.

Strong vigorous buds shooting from the base of an established blackberry plant.

to prune out the tip of any cane which is showing signs of die-back or frost damage. As the new growth develops tie it loosely in the central space of the fan, avoiding all contact with the fruit-bearing growth.

Raspberries

Summer-Fruiting Cultivars – Formative Pruning

Immediately after planting the new canes, prune them back to about 30cm (1ft) above soil level. This will encourage strong vigorous shoots to emerge from the base of the new plant and will speed up establishment.

Summer-Fruiting Cultivars – Routine Pruning and Training

Once the new canes have established and are growing vigorously (usually by midsummer), the old canes are cut out (these were the canes which were shortened when planted).

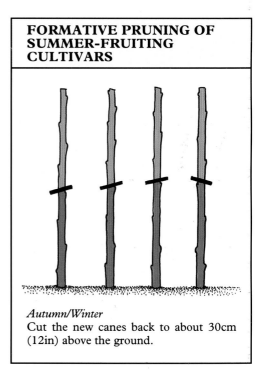

FORMATIVE PRUNING OF SUMMER-FRUITING CULTIVARS

Autumn/Winter
Cut the new canes back to about 30cm (12in) above the ground.

ROUTINE PRUNING AND TRAINING OF
SUMMER-FRUITING CULTIVARS

Summer
Soon after harvest, cut back all fruit-bearing canes to soil level. Tie in the new growth, space them 10cm (4in) apart and discard all shoots less than 1m (3.3ft) high.

Autumn/Winter
Loop any tall canes over the top wire and tie them into position.

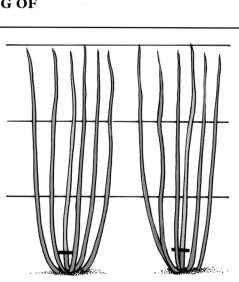

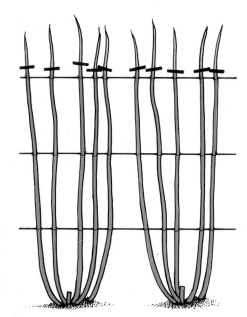

Spring
Tip the canes to 15cm (6in) above the top support wire. Any canes with frost damage should be cut back to healthy wood.

Fastening in the tip growths of summer-fruiting raspberries.

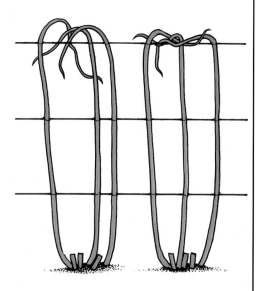

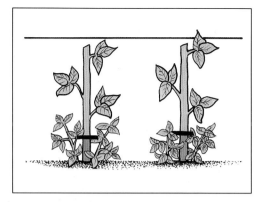

Remove the old stems to encourage rapid development of the new growth.

Regular pruning is essential to maintain high yields, as the fruit is produced on shoots which developed the previous season. Raspberries should have all the fruited canes removed at ground level immediately after harvest and all damaged and thin, weak canes cut out so that the remainder receive as much room as possible. The new shoots are usually a light brown colour, two-year-old wood is grey, with the oldest wood being dark brown.

The following spring, tip the canes to 15cm (6in) above the top support wire. Any canes with frost damage on the tips should be cut back to healthy wood. Cut out some of the canes from overcrowded sections of the row, plus any growing more than 22cm (9in) from the centre of the row.

Autumn-Fruiting Cultivars – Formative Pruning

Immediately after planting the new canes, prune all stems to one bud above soil level to speed up establishment. The next year,

Established raspberry canes during winter, well pruned and evenly spaced.

remove any thin, weak or distorted shoots.

BUSH FRUITS

Blackcurrants

The majority of the fruit is produced on shoots formed the previous year, and in order to promote the production of new shoots, hard pruning on a regular basis is essential.

Formative Pruning
Immediately after planting the new bushes, prune back all stems to one bud above soil level to speed up establishment. The following year, remove any thin, weak or distorted shoots.

Routine Pruning – Established Bushes
A system of renewal pruning in mid-winter is used for blackcurrants. This involves cutting out up to 30 per cent of the shoots, plus any thin, weak or diseased shoots. The

---

FORMATIVE PRUNING

Autumn/Winter
Cut the new canes back to one bud above the ground.

Autumn-Fruiting Cultivars – Routine Pruning and Training

Autumn-fruiting cultivars are pruned in late winter by cutting back all the canes to ground level. The new canes grow through the spring and summer, before fruiting in the autumn. In subsequent years, established plants are pruned in early winter.

Tie in the new canes, spacing them evenly 8–10cm (3–4in) apart.

ROUTINE PRUNING AND TRAINING OF AUTUMN-FRUITING CULTIVARS

Winter
Cut all canes to ground level.

Spring/Summer
Tie in the new growths, space them 10cm (4in) apart and discard all shoots less than 1m (3.3ft) high.

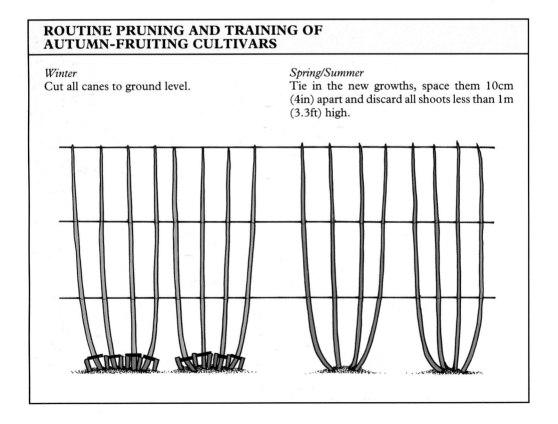

FORMATIVE PRUNING OF BLACKCURRANTS

First Year

Winter/Spring
Prune all stems to one bud above soil level, immediately after planting the new bushes.

Second Year

Autumn/Winter
Any thin, weak or small shoots are cut back hard to encourage strong, vigorous growth.

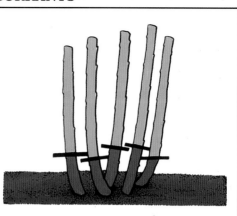

growth which should be removed is the oldest, easily identified by its colour as it is normally black, whereas the young shoots are a pale brown by the time the leaves have fallen. Using this renewal system of pruning, the entire top growth of the bush is replaced over a three-year period.

Pruning out blackcurrant shoots infested with blackcurrant gall mite (note the typically swollen big buds where the mites are feeding).

ESTABLISHED BLACK-CURRANTS – ROUTINE PRUNING

Winter
Cut out the oldest (blackest) shoots, this is usually one third of the total number of stems. At the same time remove any thin, weak or diseased shoots.

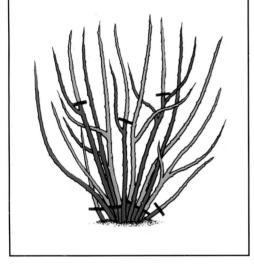

Renovation Pruning
For neglected bushes, which have not been pruned regularly and need rejuvenating, a more drastic pruning regime is needed. A greater proportion of the older wood is removed and only the branches which have developed strong, new shoots are kept. This drastic pruning may need to be repeated for a second year until all of the old (black) stems have been replaced with younger ones, but one year's crop will be lost. The new shoots which develop may need thinning to reduce competition. Only the strongest should be retained.

Gooseberries, Redcurrants and White Currants

Gooseberries, red and white currants produce fruit on short spurs which are developed by pruning back the lateral branches (side shoots). This means they can be grown in a number of shapes or forms. They are most commonly grown as bushes with an open centre, as spacing the fruiting stems aids ripening and makes picking easier. They can also be trained on a supporting framework of posts and wires as cordons, or, in the case of gooseberries, as standards.

Formative Pruning
These bushes should have a 'leg' or clear stem to prevent any branches or fruit trailing on the ground. Remove any branches which are less than 20cm (8in) above ground level to produce a short leg, and shorten the remaining shoots by half in late winter. The following winter, cut back all of the new growth by

Removing frost-damaged growth from a gooseberry in late spring.

FORMATIVE PRUNING

First Year

Winter/Spring
Immediately after planting the new bushes, cut out any shoots lower than 20cm (8in) above ground level.

Prune back all remaining stems to half their original length.

Second Year

Autumn/Winter
Any thin, weak or small shoots are cut back hard to a single bud. All the new growth is cut back by half to form the main branches.

ESTABLISHED BUSHES – ROUTINE PRUNING

Winter
Cut out the old, unproductive shoots, and remove any thin, weak or diseased shoots. Remove low-growing, over-crowded and crossing shoots, and tip each shoot.

half to form the framework of main branches. Any side shoots growing into the centre of the bush or in a downward direction are pruned back to a single bud.

Routine Pruning
Prune established bushes by removing low-growing, over-crowded and crossing shoots, to keep the centre of the bush open. This helps the fruit to ripen and makes picking easier, as well as allowing good air circulation through the plant, which helps to reduce the incidence of pests and diseases. Any side-shoots which are cut

back should be pruned to one bud to form fruiting spurs.

Cut out any old, non-fruiting shoots, and encourage strong, young shoots to grow into the available space.

CORDONS

Formative Pruning

These plants are usually trained on wires placed at 60cm (2ft) and 1.2m (4ft) above ground level, so they can grow into a vertical position, and are often referred to as 'vertical cordons'. The vigorous main shoot of a one-year-old plant is trained in a vertical position, using a bamboo cane as a guide. Start by pruning this main shoot back to half its original length in the winter, and cut back all other shoots to a single bud.

In the following summer, as the new growth develops, cut these new laterals back to five leaves. The following winter, the leader is tipped by removing the end quarter of the new growth, and the laterals are cut back even further, to two buds.

Routine Pruning

In midsummer, as the new growth develops, cut the new laterals back to five leaves. During the winter, cut back all the lateral shoots to two buds to encourage spur formation, and remove any shoots which develop close to the ground. When the main shoot or leader reaches the top of the cane, prune its new growth back each year to a single bud.

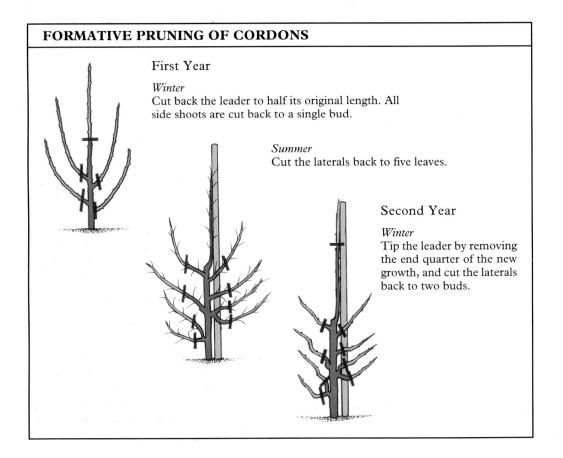

FORMATIVE PRUNING OF CORDONS

First Year

Winter
Cut back the leader to half its original length. All side shoots are cut back to a single bud.

Summer
Cut the laterals back to five leaves.

Second Year

Winter
Tip the leader by removing the end quarter of the new growth, and cut the laterals back to two buds.

ROUTINE PRUNING OF CORDONS

Summer
Cut the laterals back to five leaves.

Winter
Prune the leader back to a single bud when it reaches the top of the cane. All side shoots are cut back to two buds.

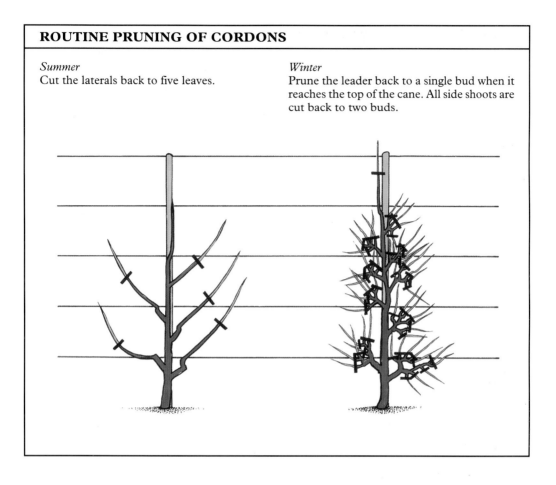

STANDARD FORMS

The cultivars to be grown as standards are the same as those grown for bushes and cordons, but they are grafted onto a 'leg' or stem at about 1.2m (4ft) above soil level. The 'leg' is usually a three-year old stem of *Ribes odoratum* or *R. divaricatum* both of which make a very good rootstock.

When standards are planted in their permanent cropping position they must be staked, as the rootstock is not strong enough to support the weight of the cropping cultivar unaided. This method of growing is ideal for varieties such as 'Leveller', which have a weeping habit. The long trailing branches can then be left to develop naturally.

These plants are usually purchased with a framework of branches already started, and pruning is the same as for plants grown as bushes. Any shoots which emerge from below the point where the cropping cultivar is grafted must be removed, as these are suckers and will compete with the cultivar.

Highbush Blueberries

These plants are becoming more popular because as well as their fruit, they produce attractive white flowers in the spring and a vivid display of golden-red leaves in the autumn. They prefer a cool, moist climate, but may take up to five years before cropping well, and they *must* have an acid soil with a pH of around 5.0.

FORMATIVE PRUNING OF HIGHBUSH BLUEBERRIES

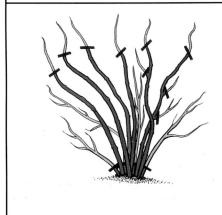

First Year

Winter
Cut back any weak shoots to a strong branch or healthy bud.

Second Year

Winter
Cut back any weak shoots to a strong branch or healthy bud.

Formative Pruning

Newly planted bushes need very little pruning for the first few years. Cut back any weak shoots in order to promote strong, vigorous growth.

Routine Pruning – Established Bushes

The fruit is produced on wood which is two or three years old and a system of renewal pruning in mid-winter is most commonly practised. This involves cutting out up to a third of the shoots, usually the oldest, which can be easily identified by their colour (normally much darker). Using this renewal system of pruning, the entire top growth of the bush is replaced over a period of three or four years. This is essential to achieve regular cropping.

ESTABLISHED BLUEBERRY BUSHES – ROUTINE PRUNING

Winter
Cut out the oldest (non-fruiting) shoots, usually one third of the stems. At the same time remove any thin, weak or diseased shoots.

CHAPTER 8

Top Fruit

Top fruit is the generic term used when referring to fruit which is produced on a tree. This group can be subdivided by the type of seed carried within the fruit. Top fruits fall into two basic categories:

1. those which produce a small pip within the fruit, such fruits as: apples, pears, figs and mulberries
2. those which produce a large stone within the fruit, such fruits as: apricots, cherries, plums and peaches.

APPLES

Spur Bearers

Apples are produced on shoots which are two years old or more and the fruits are usually borne in clusters on short spurs. Branches which are two years old will carry two types of bud: large swollen buds which produce flower clusters and then fruit, and much smaller, pointed growth buds, which form into shoots for the following year or into laterals (side shoots).

Tip Bearers

These cultivars differ in the way they bear most of their fruit. One-year-old shoots may carry fruit buds and some cultivars only produce a few spurs because they tend to bear the majority of their fruit on the tips of the branches. These 'tip-bearing cultivars' are best grown as standard, half-standard, or bush forms, because on each shoot there are

areas of bare, unproductive wood. This limits the cropping capacity of the tree, and they need renewal pruning once established.

Fruit trees can be grown in a variety of ways but usually fall into one of two categories: either free-standing trees or trained trees.

Free-standing trees are the tree and bush forms of fruit which are not trained against a wall, fence or other structure, although a tree stake may be used to provide stability after planting.

The Bush

Most commonly grown on a 75cm (2.5ft) clear stem. An open-centred branch system provides space between the fruiting branches to aid ripening and make picking easier. The bush is fairly simple to maintain and is a good tree shape for larger gardens where there is room for them to grow.

Formative Pruning
Starting with a maiden tree, the laterals (feathers) will form the first framework branches. Cut back the main central leader to a strong lateral 60–75cm (24–30in) above soil level, soon after planting. Leave two or three evenly spaced lateral branches radiating out (rather like the spokes of a wheel). All other laterals are removed.

These laterals will form the basis of the branch framework. Reduce their length by about two-thirds, cutting close to an upward-pointing bud. In the second winter, select several well-spaced growths arising from the original laterals to build up the branch framework, and shorten them by

FORMATIVE PRUNING

First Year

Winter
Prune the leader back to a selected lateral, choose three laterals to be retained and cut them back by two thirds of their original length.

Second Year

Winter
Cut back lateral and sub-lateral branches to half of their original length. Any shoots not required for the branch framework are cut back to four buds.

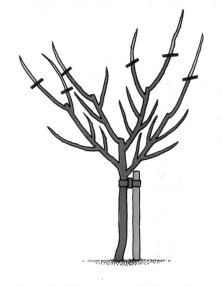

half, cutting to outward-facing buds. Any branches which are not needed for the framework are shortened to four or five buds, and all other shoots crossing the open centre are removed.

As growth continues in the second summer, remove any vigorous, upright shoots to keep a balanced shape to the tree. By the third winter, the main branch framework should be determined. The aim should be a framework of eight to ten main branches as well as several lateral branches.

Routine Pruning
Most tree and bush forms require moderate pruning in winter to stimulate growth for the next season's fruit and to maintain an

A typical pyramid tree in early spring after pruning.

ROUTINE PRUNING (SPUR BEARERS)

Winter
Cut back the branch leaders to one-third of their original length and prune back the new laterals to five buds. Thin out any spur systems which become overcrowded, and remove any old, weak or downward facing spurs.

Half-Standard and Standard

This type of tree is only really suitable for the larger garden, as they usually develop an open spreading habit and demand a lot of room.

Formative Pruning
Several years of formative pruning are needed to produce an half-standard tree with a clear stem of 1.2–1.5m (4–5ft), or a clear stem of 1.8–2.1m (6–7ft) for a standard. After planting a maiden tree, tie in the leading shoot to a cane and cut any lateral branches (feathers) back to 2.5cm (1in) in winter.

open, well-balanced structure. This will also ensure that they crop well on a regular basis and that the fruit is of good quality.

Once the framework is established, only winter pruning will be necessary for bushes. The pruning required will vary from one year to the next, depending on the type of tree growth and amount of growth made, and also the habit of the tree (whether the cultivar is predominantly spur or tip bearing). The spur bearer requires spur thinning and pruning, whereas the tip bearer is pruned using the renewal technique.

ROUTINE PRUNING (TIP BEARERS)

Winter
Cut out about a quarter of the oldest fruit-bearing stems to encourage the formation of new fruit-bearing branches. Thin out sub-lateral branches in the centre of the bush to prevent overcrowding.

FORMATIVE PRUNING OF HALF-STANDARD AND STANDARD

First Year

Winter
Cut any laterals back to 2.5cm (1in).

Spring/Summer
Cut back any lateral branches to a cluster of five leaves.

Second Year

Winter
Cut any new laterals back to 2.5cm (1in), and remove most of the lower laterals. Cut back the leader to the required height.

Spring/Summer
Cut back any lateral branches to a cluster of five leaves.

Periodically cut back lateral branches to a cluster of leaves during the spring and summer – important for helping to thicken the main stem. This procedure is repeated again in the second year, to build a strong sturdy stem. The following winter, remove most of the lower lateral branches and cut back the leader to the required height, depending on

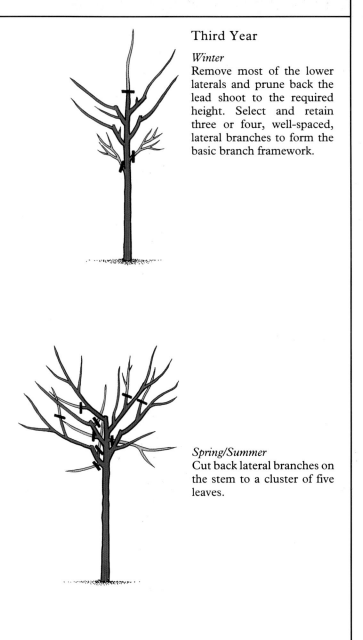

Third Year

Winter
Remove most of the lower laterals and prune back the lead shoot to the required height. Select and retain three or four, well-spaced, lateral branches to form the basic branch framework.

Spring/Summer
Cut back lateral branches on the stem to a cluster of five leaves.

Several lateral branches should then be allowed to develop below the top bud. Select and retain three or four well-spaced, lateral branches to form the basic branch framework. Training is then the same as for an open-centred bush. Subsequent pruning of the tree is also the same as for the pruning of a bush, bearing in mind that the growth will be stronger, because the tree is grafted onto a rootstock which is much more vigorous than those used for bushes. Regulated pruning is usually practised on the established tree; in most cases it is only necessary to prune hard if the tree is not making satisfactory growth.

Routine Pruning
Regulated pruning is based on the removal of shoots and occasionally sections of large crossing branches to prevent them rubbing. Thin out overcrowded laterals and sub-laterals, particularly those in the centre of the tree, to keep the branch framework open. This method of pruning is usually practised on an established tree, and it is only necessary to prune hard if the tree is not making satisfactory growth. Regulated pruning is better suited to varieties which are naturally very vigorous, particularly triploids such as 'Bramley Seedling', 'Blenheim Orange', and 'Jonagold'.

whether the tree is destined to be either a standard, or half-standard. To form a standard, the tree will need to grow for a third year to achieve the required height.

ROUTINE PRUNING OF HALF-STANDARD AND STANDARD

Winter
Remove crossing or rubbing branches, thin out overcrowded laterals and sub-laterals. This will encourage the development of new shoots.

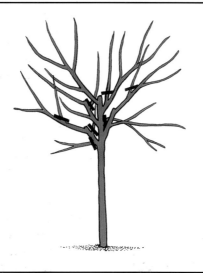

A well-pruned open-centred apple tree in early spring.

Bark Ringing

A technique called bark ringing can be used as a last resort to curb shoot growth and induce a greater fruit set. Remove a narrow band of bark from around the trunk through to the cambium layer at a height of about 1m (3ft) above soil level during the late spring, and cover the wound with waterproof tape. This restricts the passage of nutrients and plant hormones between the top

BARK-RINGING

Spring
Place a tape or string around the trunk of the tree as a guide, make two parallel cuts up to 1cm (½in) apart. Carefully remove the ring of bark between the two parallel cuts and cover the open wound with tape to protect it from infection.

Summer/Autumn
Remove the tape when the wound has healed.

growth and the roots, and these chemicals become concentrated in the above-ground part of the tree.

Bark-ringing is a very risky procedure which must be carried out carefully and correctly or the tree may die. However, it can be very effective on over-vigorous trees which produce copious amounts of shoot growth and unsatisfactory crops of fruit.

The wound should heal over by the autumn, when the waterproof tape may be removed. The following year, the tree should produce much larger amounts of blossom and, consequently, a much heavier crop of fruit because the reaction of many wounded plants is to produce large quantities of seed to ensure the survival of the species.

Spindle Bush

The spindle bush form of tree was first developed in Germany before the Second World War. The tree is trained into a cone shape which, when laden with fruit, looks rather like a Christmas tree covered in decorations. The whole idea behind this shape is that all of the fruit are exposed to the sunlight for ripening and can be picked without having to use a ladder.

Once the basic framework is established, only renewal pruning and training to retain the overall shape are required. Commercial fruit growers have developed a number of variations to the spindle bush, but the basic concept remains the same. That is, to develop the three or four lowest branches as a cropping platform bearing the bulk of the fruit. This is achieved by cutting out any shoots which would otherwise develop in the centre of the tree. Shoots which develop higher in the tree are allowed to produce fruit and are then pruned back severely, to be replaced by fresh growth.

Formative Pruning
Starting with a maiden tree, support it with a 2m (6ft) stake, and the laterals (feathers) will form the first branches of the framework. Cut back the main central leader to a strong lateral, 60–90cm (24–36in) above soil level, soon after planting. Leave two or three evenly spaced lateral branches radiating out (rather like the spokes of a wheel). All other laterals are removed.

Towards the end of the first summer, any strong growths are tied down into an horizontal position, to discourage shoot growth and encourage the tree to fruit. If growth is weak, this tying is not necessary.

In the second summer, tie down the lateral branches to the base of the stake supporting the tree at an angle of 30 degrees using strong string. For long branches, use more than one tie if necessary.

Very vigorous shoots growing upwards from the main stem and any laterals are removed. Tie the main stem to the support stake in order to keep it growing vertically.

As the tree develops, cut the main stem back by one third of its original length, and remove the strings from the horizontal lateral branches (once the wood matures these branches will be 'set' into position). By the following summer, a new layer of branches can be tied into position, forming a second tier of horizontal branches, but try to avoid the upper tier shading the lower tier. Those shoots not selected for tying down are cut back to a single bud.

FORMATIVE PRUNING OF SPINDLE BUSH

First Year

Winter
Prune the leader back to 90cm (3ft) above the ground. Cut back about four strong laterals to half their original length and remove all other laterals.

Summer
Cut out any vigorous upright shoots as they form.

Tie down the four laterals into an horizontal position.

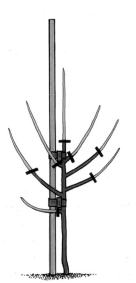

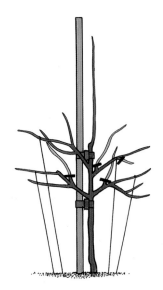

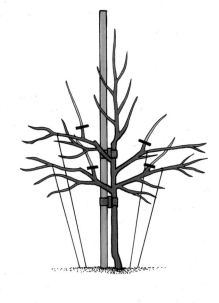

Second Year

Winter
Prune the leader back to one-third of the current season's growth. Cut back four strong laterals to half their original length and remove other young laterals.

Summer
Cut out any vigorous upright shoots as they form.

Tie down the four laterals into an horizontal position.

By the third winter, cut the main stem back by on-third of its original length again and remove the strings from the horizontal lateral branches.

In the third summer, a new layer of branches can be tied into position, forming a third tier of horizontal branches, but again, try to avoid the upper tier shading the lower tiers. Those shoots which are not selected for tying down are cut back to a single bud. Fruit will be forming on the lowest tier of horizontal branches.

Routine Pruning
Renewal pruning is appropriate for spindle bushes and involves the annual reduction or removal of a proportion of the older, fruiting shoots to their base in order to stimulate the growth of new, young wood. Keep the central stem of a spindle clear by pruning out any vigorous growth which may be crossing or shading other laterals. The aim is to have all the branches well-spaced and radiating out from the central stem. If the central leader becomes too vigorous, it may dominate the tree. To avoid this, remove it, and replace it with an upward-growing lateral shoot.

PEARS

Pears have similar pruning requirements to apples and often the same techniques are used for both. However, once they have started to produce fruit on a regular basis, pears will tolerate much harder pruning. Spur production is much more prolific on pears, and spur thinning is a regular task on most cultivars. They tend to have a more vigorous growth habit than apples and although they can be grown as bushes or occasionally, standards or half-standards in just the same way, the most popular form is the dwarf pyramid.

The Dwarf Pyramid

Pears are commonly grown as dwarf pyramids with a central stem. This is to space the fruiting branches evenly in order to aid ripening and make picking easier.

Formative Pruning
Start by planting a feathered maiden tree in late autumn or early winter. As soon as the buds start to grow in the spring, cut the main stem back to a height of about 50–75cm (20–30in). Shorten any side shoots to 15cm (6in), or to five good buds, and remove any weak or broken laterals. Cut back all new lateral growth to five leaves in midsummer.

ROUTINE PRUNING OF SPINDLE BUSH

Winter
Prune out the sub-laterals from the lower tiers of branches if they are unproductive or overcrowded.

Any large unproductive branches in the upper tiers are cut back hard to a single bud.

FORMATIVE PRUNING OF PEARS

First Year

Winter
Cut back the leader just above a bud, between 50–75cm (20–30in) above ground level. Prune the laterals back to 15cm (6in) and remove any unwanted laterals.

Summer
Cut back new lateral growth to five buds and any sub-laterals back to three leaves. Remove any blossom.

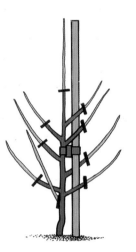

Second Year

Winter
Cut back the current season's growth to leave about 25cm (10in).

Summer
Cut back new lateral growth to five buds and any sub-laterals back to three leaves. Remove any blossom.

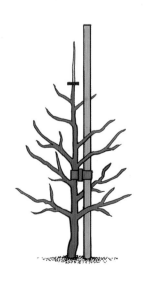

In the following winter, shorten the leader to leave some 25cm (10in) of new growth, cutting to a bud pointing in the opposite direction to that of the bud chosen the previous spring to help keep the leader straight. Cut back laterals to 15–20cm (6–8in) to a downward- or outward-facing bud.

During the first few years, remove any blossom which forms on the central leader, as lateral branches, not fruits, are what are required here.

Routine Pruning

In subsequent summers, cut back lateral branch leaders to five leaves beyond the basal cluster of leaves. Laterals emerging directly from the branches are cut back to three leaves. Those arising from existing spurs are cut back to one leaf beyond a basal cluster.

In subsequent winters, cut back the central leader to leave 20–25cm (8–10in) of the current season's growth. Cut back to a single bud any secondary growths which may have grown as a result of summer pruning.

When the trees have achieved the required height, restrict their growth by cutting the central leader back to a single bud of the current season's growth. This should be done in early summer. Any other shoots needing restriction, such as those arising from the top of the tree or branch leaders growing into adjacent trees, can be treated in the same way. Any thinning out of branches or spurs is best done in winter.

Strong healthy fruit buds and spurs on a dormant pear tree.

ROUTINE PRUNING OF THE DWARF PYRAMID

Summer
Cut back new, lateral growth to five buds, any sub-laterals back to three leaves. Cut the central leader back to a single bud when the tree reaches the required height.

Winter
Spur thinning may be required to prevent overcrowding, and remove the older wood to promote the younger.

PLUMS

Plums form their fruit on two-year-old wood, at the base of one-year-old wood and on fruiting spurs. Once they have started to produce fruit on a regular basis, plums require very little pruning if grown as free-standing trees. The shoot growth of plums naturally tends to become congested as the tree ages and regulated pruning in the summer is used to keep the plant fruiting.

Plums tend to have a lax, spreading habit. Although they can be grown as bushes or occasionally standards or half-standards, as the average garden becomes smaller, the most popular free-standing tree form is the pyramid.

The Plum Pyramid

Plums may be grown as pyramids with a central stem, this is to space evenly the fruiting branches in order to aid ripening and make picking easier.

Formative Pruning
Start by planting a tall, feathered maiden tree in late autumn or early winter, providing a strong stake for support. As soon as the buds start to grow in the spring, cut the main stem back to a height of about 1.5m (5ft), shorten any side shoots to five good buds and remove any laterals from the bottom 45cm (18in) of the stem.

Cut back all new lateral growth to five leaves in midsummer, and reduce the sub-laterals to three leaves. These cuts should be made to a downward-facing bud, to encourage growth in an horizontal direction. The central leader is tied to the stake; any vigorous competing laterals are cut out.

In the following spring, shorten the leader to leave 25cm (10in) of new growth, cutting to a bud pointing in the opposite direction from that of the bud chosen the previous spring to help keep the leader straight.

In the summer, cut back lateral growths to 15–20cm (6–8in) and reduce the sub-laterals to three leaves, cutting to a downward- or outward-facing bud.

During the first few years remove any blossom which forms on the central leader, as lateral branches, not fruits, are what are required here.

Routine Pruning
In subsequent summers, cut back lateral branches which compete with the central leader, prune back lateral shoots to five leaves beyond the basal cluster of leaves, and cut back any laterals emerging directly from the branches to three leaves.

When the trees have achieved the required height of 2–2.5m (6–8ft), restrict their growth by cutting the central leader back to

FORMATIVE PRUNING OF THE PLUM PYRAMID

First Year

Spring
Cut back the leader to just above a bud at 1.5m (5ft) above ground level. Prune the laterals back to 15cm (6in) and remove any unwanted laterals from the bottom 45cm (18in).

Summer
Cut back new lateral growth to five leaves, and any sub-laterals back to three leaves. Remove any blossom.

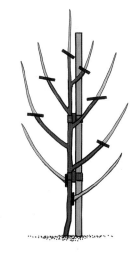

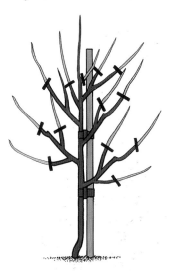

Cutting out a crossing branch which is damaging a neighbouring branch by rubbing against it.

Second Year

Spring
Cut back the current season's growth on the central leader to leave about 25cm (10in) of new growth.

Summer
Cut back new lateral growth to five buds, and any sub-laterals back to three leaves. Remove any blossom.

ROUTINE PRUNING OF THE PLUM PYRAMID

Summer
Cut back new, lateral growth to five leaves, and any sub-laterals to three leaves. Cut the central leader back to a single bud when the tree reaches the required height. Spur thinning may be required to prevent overcrowding. Remove the older wood to promote younger growth.

a single bud in early summer. Any other shoots needing restriction, such as those arising from the top of the tree or branch leaders growing into adjacent trees, can be treated in the same way. Any thinning out of branches or spurs is best done in the summer.

TRAINED TREES

Trained trees are those which are grown with the aid of support, be it a wall, fence or some other means of support. The main aims of growing trained trees are to produce a large number of high-quality fruits from a relatively confined space, and to provide shelter and protection for those fruiting plants which are not fully hardy.

The most commonly encountered forms are cordon, espalier and fan.

Once their branch framework is established, trained trees need to be pruned (mainly in summer) to maintain shape, curb vegetative growth, and stimulate the production of fruit buds.

The Oblique Cordon

Formative Pruning
In the winter immediately after planting a feathered maiden tree at an angle of 45 degrees, cut back all the lateral shoots (feathers) to 10cm (4in). Much of the pruning will be carried out through the summer, with most of the shoots being pruned in succession as they mature.

Routine Pruning
In order to keep trained trees producing a constant supply of fruit buds, and to suppress vigorous shoot growth, most of the pruning is carried out in the summer. Once the young shoots have become woody at the base, all new, lateral branches growing directly from the main stem or a main branch are cut back to three leaves above the basal cluster. Side shoots growing from spurs and existing laterals are pruned back to just one leaf above the basal cluster of leaves. This is a constant job through the summer as the shoots mature over a period of time.

Sometimes, after summer pruning, secondary side shoots develop below the pruning cut. To prevent this, leave a small number of the longer shoots unpruned (about every tenth shoot). These shoots are then tied in securely to other branches so that they are roughly horizontal. This has the effect of drawing the sap down, and discouraging this secondary growth from developing. Do not prune any of these shoots until after fruiting, they can then be cut back to a single bud. The standard method of summer pruning is called the Modified Lorette System.

FORMATIVE PRUNING OF THE OBLIQUE CORDON

First Year

Winter

Plant a feathered maiden at an angle, with the graft union facing upwards. Cut back all laterals to four buds, leave all laterals of less than 10cm (4in) unpruned.

Summer

As the bases of the new lateral shoots become woody, prune each back to three buds. Prune any sub-laterals to a single bud. When the main stem reaches above the top support wire, cut it back to a bud just above the wire.

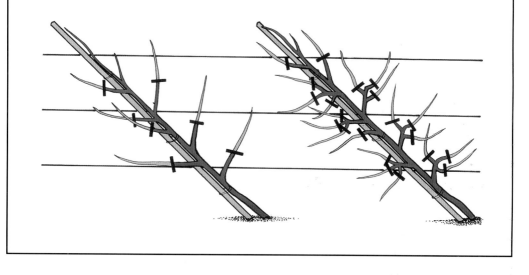

As a tree ages, the spurs may become entangled and carry small, poorly coloured fruit. Some spur thinning may then be required to prevent overcrowding when spur systems become congested. Remove the older wood in favour of the younger. In time it may become necessary to saw off whole spur systems to allow room for new ones to develop.

The Espalier

This tree form is based on producing and training a series of two or three tiers of horizontal shoots grown in pairs at right angles to the main stem.

The tiers are trained along horizontal wires set about 40cm (16in) apart. Top fruits most commonly grown as espaliers include apples and pears.

Formative Pruning

Start by planting a maiden whip (no feathers) in late autumn or early winter. After planting, or as soon as the buds start to grow, cut the main stem back to a bud just above the lowest horizontal wire. Ideally, find a place where three healthy buds are located close together, to form the first three shoots. When growth starts, actually rub out any buds which are not required.

In the first summer, train the shoot growing from the top bud vertically upwards, and tie it to a cane fastened to the wires for this purpose. Train the shoots from the two lower buds to an angle of 45 degrees. If one shoot grows slower than the other, raise it to a more vertical position.

At the end of the growing season, lower these shoots and tie them to the horizontal wire. Any other shoots growing from the

ROUTINE PRUNING OF THE OBLIQUE CORDON

Winter
Thin out old congested spurs.

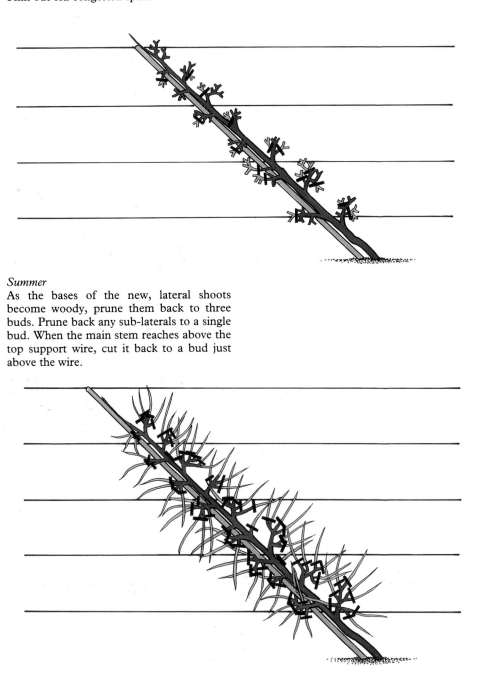

Summer
As the bases of the new, lateral shoots become woody, prune them back to three buds. Prune back any sub-laterals to a single bud. When the main stem reaches above the top support wire, cut it back to a bud just above the wire.

FORMATIVE PRUNING OF THE ESPALIER

First Year

Winter
After planting a maiden whip, cut back the main stem to a bud just above the lowest horizontal wire.

Summer
Train the top bud vertically upwards and tie it to a cane fastened to the wires. Train the shoots from the two lower buds along canes at an angle of 45 degrees.

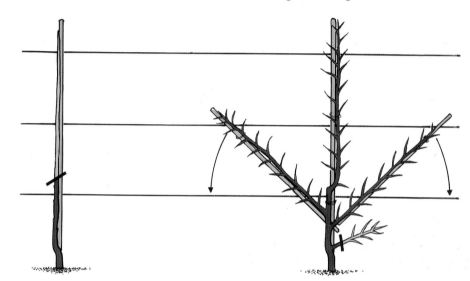

Second Year

Winter
Cut back the main stem to a bud just above the second horizontal wire. Lower the lateral shoots and tie them to the horizontal wire. Any other shoots growing from the central stem should be pruned back to 10cm (4in).

(continued overleaf)

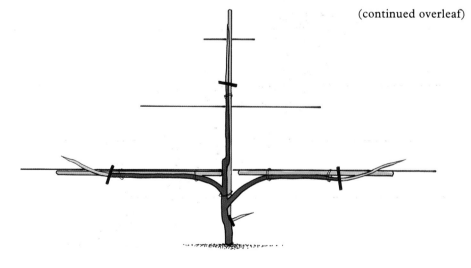

FORMATIVE PRUNING OF THE ESPALIER

(continued)

Summer

Train the top bud vertically upwards and tie it to a cane fastened to the wires. Train the shoots from the two lower buds along canes at an angle of 45 degrees. Sub-laterals of over 20cm (8in) long which form on the horizontal branches, are cut back to four buds. Once a tier has reached required length, prune back the leading shoot to a single bud.

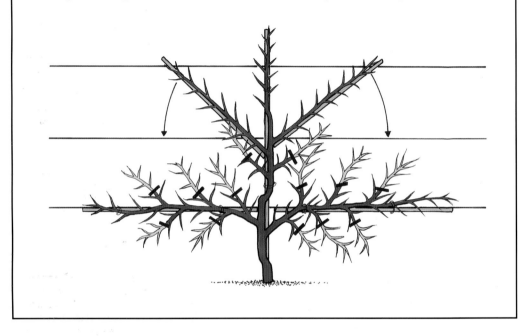

central stem should be pruned back to 10cm (4in).

In the second and subsequent winters, the same process is repeated until the central stem has reached the required height. At this stage, only two lateral shoots are allowed to develop from the vertical leader. These are trained in opposite directions along the top wire.

The leading shoot of each tier is left unpruned unless growth has been poor and the stimulus of winter pruning is required. If this is necessary, tip the previous summer's growth by one third, pruning to a bud facing in the required direction. Once a tier has reached the required length, prune back the leading shoot to a single bud in early summer.

In the second and subsequent summers, starting in early July, this process is repeated, with the three new shoots arising from the vertical stem being treated in the same way as those in the first year.

The leading shoots from existing tiers are also tied down, taking care not to tie them down into a horizontal position too early or extension growth will be checked.

The current season's lateral growths (side shoots) which are growing directly from the tiers or spurs, and spurs growing from the central stem, should be summer-pruned.

Nicking and Notching

Sometimes it may be necessary to correct the balance of the branch framework on a

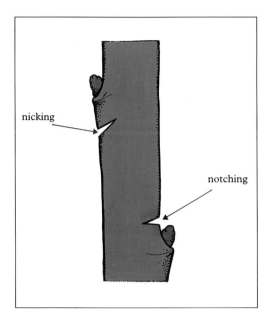

Nicking and notching can be used to manipulate bud development.

trained tree. This can be achieved by nicking, which weakens the growth of a particular bud. Make a nick or a small cut with a sharp knife just below a bud to inhibit its growth.

Notching strengthens the growth of a particular bud, and is done by making a notch just above the bud in order to increase vigour and stimulate new growth. Notching can also be used to stimulate the production of side shoots from bare lengths of stem. Nicking and notching are most effective in spring when the sap is rising.

Routine Pruning
When the horizontal arms of the top tier are established, cut back the central leader to leave just one bud of the new growth. As each tier reaches the required length, prune back the tip of the shoot to a single bud in early summer.

To keep espalier trees producing a constant supply of fruit buds, and suppress vigorous shoot growth, most of the pruning is done in the summer.

As the young shoots become woody at the base, all new lateral branches growing directly from the main stem or main branches are cut back to three leaves above the basal cluster. Side shoots growing from spurs and existing laterals are pruned back to just one bud above the basal cluster of leaves.

To prevent secondary growths forming, leave a small number of the longer shoots unpruned (about every tenth shoot). These shoots are then tied in securely to other branches so that they are roughly horizontal. This has the effect of drawing the sap down and discouraging this secondary growth from developing. Do not prune any of these shoots until after fruiting. They can then be cut back to a single bud.

THE ESPALIER – ROUTINE PRUNING

Winter
Thin out old, congested spurs.

Summer
As the bases of the new, lateral shoots become woody, prune them back to three buds. Prune back any sub-laterals to a single bud. When the main stem reaches above the top support wire, cut it back to a bud just above the wire.

Established spur systems which have become too crowded or complicated should be thinned or simplified in the winter and the subsequent growth pruned in the summer as described in the preceding paragraph.

The Fan

This tree form is achieved by producing and training a series of lateral shoots (ribs) and sub-laterals, to radiate out in an arc from a short leg or stem. This method is most commonly used for members of the cherry

FORMATIVE PRUNING OF THE FAN

First Year

Winter
After planting, cut back the stem to a pair of lateral branches 30cm (1ft) above the ground. Remove all other laterals, cutting them close to the main stem.

Summer
Tie the two lateral shoots to canes at an angle of 45 degrees. Tie in the new growth and any selected laterals.

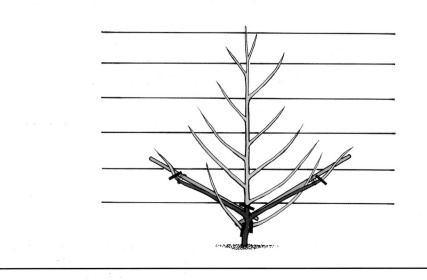

family, including acid cherries, sweet cherries, apricots, figs, peaches and plums.

Formative Pruning

A fan must have a support framework. This usually involves fixing horizontal support wires at intervals about 20cm (8in) apart, the lowest being 40cm (16in) above soil level. After planting the maiden tree and just before growth starts in the spring, cut back to a pair of lateral branches (the ribs of the fan) about 30cm (1ft) above the ground. Remove all other laterals, cutting them close to main stem.

In the first summer, when the two lateral shoots are about 30cm (1ft) long, tie them to canes placed at an angle of approximately 45 degrees or a little lower. If one shoot grows more weakly than the opposite one, it should be temporarily trained at a slightly higher angle. This will speed up its growth rate until both shoots are of a similar size. Tie in the shoot extension growth and any selected laterals.

In the second winter, cut back the two side branches (ribs) to a bud 45cm (18in) from the main stem.

In the second summer, allow the shoot from the end bud of each branch to grow on and tie it in. Also allow two suitably spaced shoots to grow on the upper side of each branch and one on the under side. These are tied to canes, and as they grow, prune out any competing shoots.

In the third winter, cut back each of the branches to leave 75cm (30in) of mature wood from the previous season's growth.

In the third summer, allow the shoot from the end bud of each branch to grow on and tie it in. Also allow two suitably spaced

FORMATIVE PRUNING OF THE FAN

Second Year

Winter
Prune back the two side branches to 45cm (18in) from the main stem.

Summer
Tie in the extension growth on each branch. Allow two shoots to grow on the upper side and one on the under side of each branch, and tie these to canes.

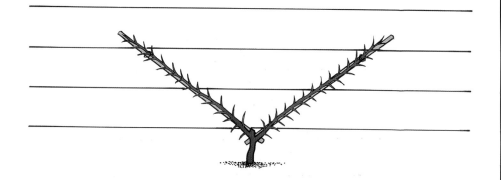

Third Year

Winter
Cut back each of the branches to 75cm (30in).

Summer
Tie in extension growth to canes. Young shoots are spaced at 10cm (4in) intervals and are tipped at 40cm (16in) long.

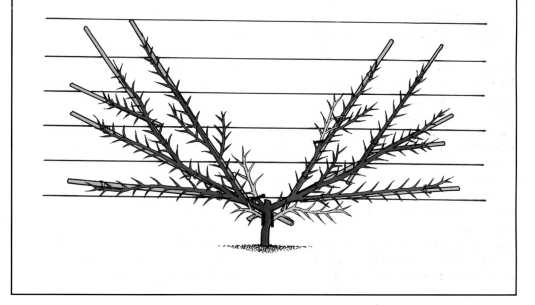

A well-formed fan-trained peach growing against a wall.

shoots to grow on the upper side of each branch and one on the under side, and tie them to canes.

Attention can now be given to fruit production. Allow the end bud on each of the eight branches to grow on and tie them in. Allow young shoots to grow out from the upper and lower sides of the branches, these are spaced at 10cm (4in) intervals. These growths will carry next year's fruit and are usually tipped when they reach approximately 40cm (16in) long.

Routine Pruning

The aim is to provide a constant supply of young shoots to replace the old, cropping wood. This is usually done after harvesting the fruit. The fruiting shoot is pruned out and replaced with a shoot from just below the point where the cut was made. This

ROUTINE PRUNING OF THE FAN

Summer

Select a suitable replacement and prune out each fruit-bearing shoot. Tie in the replacement shoots at 10cm (4in) intervals.

All stone fruits should be pruned in the summer whenever possible, to reduce the risk of infection from the fungus *Chondrostereum purpureum* (Silverleaf), which usually enters the tree through pruning wounds made in the winter.

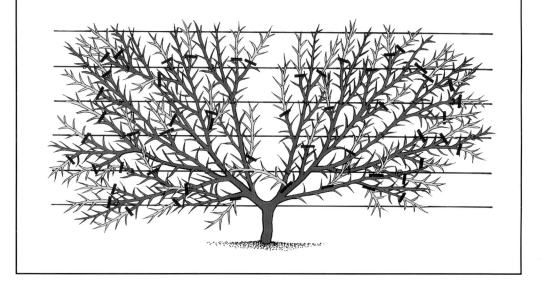

process must be carried out regularly to prevent the growth becoming congested and non-productive.

FIGS

Historians are uncertain as to where the fig first originated, but it is thought to have been brought from Asia. It is among the oldest fruits in cultivation and many credit the Romans with being the first to bring it into Britain. There are accurate records of figs being planted at Lambeth Palace in the latter half of the sixteenth century.

Figs require a warm, sunny position and, ideally, protection from severe frost. Although they can be grown as bushes, figs are most commonly grown as fan-trained trees against a wall or fence.

Formative Pruning

After planting a two-year-old tree with three or four strong branches, bend down the two lowest branches and tie them to canes placed at an angle of approximately 45° or a little lower (these will form the ribs of the fan).

In the spring, trim off all frost-damaged shoots and when the two lateral shoots are about 45cm (18in) long, cut them back by one-third to encourage replacement shoots and fruiting growth to form. Tie in the shoot extension growth and any selected laterals, and space them at least 40cm (16in) apart.

In the second spring, allow the shoot from the end bud of each branch to grow on and tie it in. Also, allow two suitably spaced shoots to grow on the upper side of each branch and one on the under side. These

FORMATIVE PRUNING OF FIGS

First Year

Spring/Summer
After planting, bend down the two branches and tie them to canes. Trim off frost-damaged shoots and cut back two lateral shoots to encourage replacement shoots to form. Tie in the shoot extension growth and laterals.

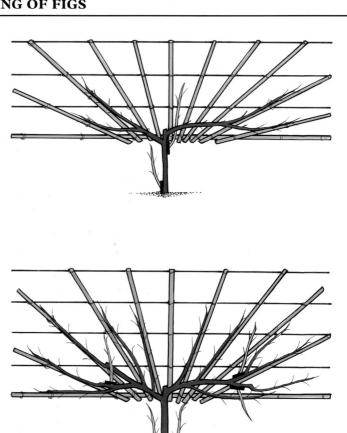

Second Year

Spring/Summer
Tie in the extension growth from the end bud of each branch. Allow two suitably spaced shoots (40cm (16in) apart) to grow on the upper side of each branch and one on the under side, tie these to canes. Cut back a number of the old, bare branches.

are tied to canes. As they grow, prune out any competing shoots. Cut back a proportion of the old, bare branches to a single bud to promote new growth.

Routine Pruning

The aim is to provide a constant supply of young shoots to replace the old cropping wood. This is usually done in the spring.

Some of the younger shoots are pruned back to a single bud to produce fresh growth along the main framework of branches. As the young shoots become woody at the base, all new lateral branches growing directly from the main stem or main branches are cut back to five leaves. This process must be carried out regularly to prevent the growth becoming congested and non-productive.

ROUTINE PRUNING OF FIGS

Spring
Prune back some of the younger shoots to a single bud to produce fresh growth along the branches.

Summer
All new lateral branches on the main stem are cut back to five leaves. This will encourage fruits to form on these short branches.

CHAPTER 9

Trees

Trees give more of a sense of permanence and maturity to a garden than any other group of plants we grow. Because of this impression of permanence it is easy to assume that they can grow forever, and require little or no care or attention. In nature, to a certain extent, this is true, but a garden is not a natural environment, it is one which is often highly managed and contrived, and the plants within it reflect this management process.

In an ornamental situation, correct pruning and training is used to control a tree's strength and vigour, and ultimately, to extend its life. It is also a means of controlling the growth, shape and size of the tree, and in some instances, even enhancing the ornamental qualities. For example, *Populus × candicans* 'Aurora' is a conspicuously variegated tree, with creamy-white, pink-edged leaves. However, this attractive colouring appears only on the younger leaves. In order to achieve the maximum impact from this tree, the branches must be cut back hard to encourage these brightly coloured juvenile leaves to develop.

FORMATIVE PRUNING

It is important to start when the tree is young, and to prune it correctly in order to develop a strong and balanced structural framework with a straight stem and well spaced branches. Careful, well-planned pruning in the early formative years will have long-term benefits for the health and vigour of the tree throughout the remainder

of its life. This is particularly important with plants such as: *Acer* (Maple), *Aesculus* (Horse chestnut), and *Fraxinus* (Ash)

Badly timed pruning stimulates the wrong type of growth.

which have their buds arranged in pairs. If the central stem is allowed to 'fork' into two stems, this can lead to the stem splitting in later years, resulting in the entire tree being lost.

The amount of pruning and training required will depend on the type and shape of tree and as well as the desired effect. For some trees, relatively little pruning is required to produce a well-balanced specimen but for others a great deal of care and attention is required.

TIMING

Most deciduous trees are pruned when they are dormant in late autumn or winter but they can be pruned at other times depending upon the reasons for pruning. However, there are exceptions, as some subjects will 'bleed' heavily (exude sap) if cut in late winter or early spring e.g. *Acer* (Maple), *Aesculus* (Horse chestnut), *Betula* (Birch) and *Juglans* (Walnut). These will all bleed extensively, often from early February onwards, and for this reason they are best pruned in the middle of summer when they are in full leaf. Most evergreen trees require little or no pruning other than the removal of any dead, damaged or diseased branches. This is best done in late summer.

THE PRINCIPLES OF PRUNING

In order to approach the task in hand competently the first stage of pruning is to remove any dead, dying, diseased or damaged wood (the four Ds). This allows you to assess the amount of live, healthy material available. The second stage is to cut out any weak or straggly shoots so that you have a pretty good idea of what is left as a potential framework to work with.

From this point, you are best able to decide which branches should be pruned back or removed to achieve well-balanced growth. Care must be taken to work with the habit of the tree rather than adopting a pruning regime which is constantly fighting the natural growth pattern of the plant you are growing.

Remember that hard pruning stimulates the production of large amounts of strong, vigorous growth, whereas light pruning will produce much more even growth of a more uniform size and vigour. Great care must be taken to ensure that all pruning cuts are accurate and precise to reduce the damage to the tree to an absolute minimum.

When cutting back a stem, always cut immediately above a healthy bud, or with certain species e.g. *Acer* (Maple) and *Aesculus* (Horse chestnut), make a straight cut with sharp secateurs directly above a pair of buds. With side shoots, cut just above a bud pointing in the intended direction of growth. If, for example, you are thinning out congested stems, cut back to an outward-facing bud or shoot, which will prevent the new growth from rubbing against other stems as it grows.

The main categories of tree are deciduous which shed their leaves in the winter, and evergreen which retain their leaves in the winter. The evergreen group can be divided into two:

1. Broad-leaved evergreens, e.g. *Ilex* (Holly)
2. Conifers, e.g. *Chamaecyparis lawsoniana* (Lawson's Cypress)

DECIDUOUS TREES

Deciduous trees come in many shapes and forms, the most common shapes being the feathered tree and the standard. The feathered tree has a natural shape with a central main stem or leader, and branches arranged from ground level up to the crown. The

A cherry tree with a forked stem; the fork being a point of structural weakness in this tree.

Over a period of time, the fork will open and the trunk of the tree will split (right).

standard tree, however, has the branches starting at 1.8m (6ft) above ground level on a stem or 'leg'.

Magnolia

Formative Pruning

With trees such as *Magnolia* early pruning is relatively straightforward. After planting, remove any shoots which compete with the main stem to prevent a 'branch fork'

FORMATIVE PRUNING

Remove any shoots competing with the main stem. Cut out any weak, thin or crossing shoots and overcrowded branches.

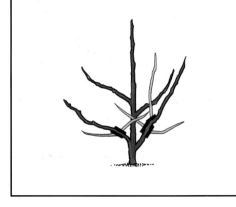

developing. Remove any weak, thin or cross-ing shoots, and thin out overcrowded branches to develop a well-balanced frame-work of branches. This process will be repeated for several years after planting.

Routine Pruning

With the large tree *Magnolias*, there are no regular pruning requirements, other than to maintain the vigour and shape of the speci-men. As it matures, the tree may become overcrowded with many thin, whippy branches in the centre. Some thinning may then be necessary. Any large branches which spoil the balance and shape of the tree should be reduced in size. Inward-growing shoots should also be removed to allow light and air into the centre of the tree.

ROUTINE PRUNING

Remove thin, whippy branches in the cen-tre of the tree and thin out overcrowded and inward growing shoots. Reduce the size of large branches spoiling the shape of the tree.

Remove or thin out any epicormic (water) shoots.

Excessively hard pruning may result in the tree producing masses of epicormic (water) shoots, and these should be removed or thinned out as they develop. For a plant such as *Magnolia*, the best time to prune is immediately after flowering.

Sorbus aucuparia (Mountain Ash)

Formative Pruning

With trees such as Mountain ash, pruning during the first three years is aimed towards

Removing large branches from the stem is often a sign of poor formative pruning.

FORMATIVE PRUNING OF MOUNTAIN ASH

First Year

Winter
After planting remove any shoots competing with the main stem.

Spring
Remove all lateral shoots from the bottom third of the tree. All lateral shoots on the middle third of the tree are cut back by half.

Second Year

Winter
The shortened laterals on the middle third of the tree are removed completely.

Spring
All lateral shoots on the next section of the tree are cut back by half.

In subsequent years this process is repeated until a clear stem of 1.8m (6ft) is achieved.

Epicormic shoots being removed from a Tilia *(lime tree)*.

producing the clear stem of the tree. After planting, remove any shoots which compete with the main stem and any thin or crossing shoots. In the first spring, prune off all lateral shoots from the bottom third of the tree. All lateral shoots on the middle third of the tree are reduced by half their length. The top third is allowed to grow unpruned.

In the early winter, the reduced lateral shoots on the middle third of the tree are removed completely. This procedure is repeated over the next two years until a clear stem of 1.8m (6ft) is achieved.

Routine Pruning

With an established ornamental tree, there are no regular pruning requirements, other than to maintain the vigour and shape of the specimen. As it matures, the tree may become overcrowded with many thin whippy branches in the centre, and some thinning may then become necessary. Any large branches which spoil the balance and shape of the tree should be reduced in size. Inward-growing shoots should also be removed to allow light and air into the centre of the tree. Excessively hard pruning may result in the tree producing masses of epicormic (water) shoots, and these should be removed or thinned out as soon as they develop.

BROAD-LEAVED EVERGREEN TREES

Only a relatively small number of broad-leaved evergreen trees are seen in our gardens. Usually they require very little training as young plants and are best treated as feathered trees.

Ilex (Holly)

Formative Pruning

A strong, main stem or central leader should be established by training a strong vertical shoot against a cane: this can be removed as the woody stem matures. Prune out any competing leaders or badly placed laterals during the early years of growth. Any pruning necessary is carried out in the spring just as the new season's growth starts.

Routine Pruning

As the tree develops further, pruning is seldom necessary and often undesirable. Regular pruning is restricted to the reduction or removal of dead, dying, diseased or damaged branches. With some variegated holly cultivars, 'reverted' shoots that are either all green or all cream in colour can be cut out. The attractive, billowing outlines of trees such as *Quercus ilex* (Holm or ever-

---

ROUTINE PRUNING

Winter
Remove thin, whippy branches in the centre of the tree, and thin out overcrowded and inward growing shoots. Reduce the size of large branches spoiling the shape of the tree.

Summer
Remove any shoots which develop on the stem of the tree.

FORMATIVE PRUNING OF HOLLY

First Year

Winter
After planting remove any strong shoots competing with the main stem. Train a strong, vertical shoot against a cane.

Spring
Prune the shoot tips to encourage branching.

In subsequent years this process is repeated until the tree reaches the required height.

ROUTINE PRUNING

Spring
Remove any dead, dying, diseased or damaged branches. Lightly trim the tips of shoots to encourage branching.

Summer
Remove any 'reverted' shoots which develop on the tree.

green oak) can be ruined by attempts to prune them formally and they are best left to their own devices unless any problems should emerge.

CONIFERS

Chamaecyparis (Cypress)

Formative Pruning

The basic growth pattern of conifers, such as cypress, fir and pine is for a single central leader to grow with whorls of branches developing at fairly regular intervals along its length. They should be left to grow naturally, pruning or training only becomes necessary if the shoots are damaged.

Routine Pruning
Sometimes the leader or the terminal bud dies and one or more shoots from the top

FORMATIVE PRUNING

First Year

Spring
After planting remove any strong shoots competing with the growing point. Train a strong, vertical shoot against a cane if necessary. Prune the lateral shoot tips to encourage branching and even growth.

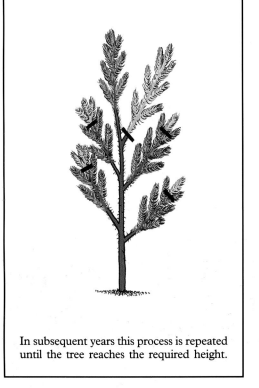

In subsequent years this process is repeated until the tree reaches the required height.

ROUTINE PRUNING

Spring
Remove any dead, dying, diseased or damaged branches. Lightly trim the tips of shoots to encourage branching. Remove any 'reverted' shoots which develop on variegated trees.

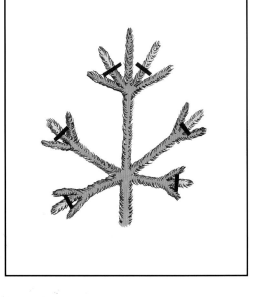

Any pruning of mature conifers should be restricted to removing only entirely dead branches. Attempts to reduce them in height normally prove unsatisfactory and frequently leave ugly, mutilated plants which are best dug up and burned.

Several evergreens such as *Taxus* (Yew), *Chamaecyparis* (Cypress) and *Thuja* (Western Red Cedar) make excellent hedge plants and tolerate clipping as young plants. Unlike broad-leaved trees, true conifers (not yew) do not normally re-grow from mature wood as there are few or no dormant buds present in the older woody branches and stems.

POLLARDING

This is a severe pruning technique which can be used for a variety of reasons:

whorl will begin to replace it naturally. The problem here is that two branches will often compete and a forked head may develop, the fork is a weak point and the tree may split when it is older.

As soon as the need for a new leader is identified, the best-placed strong shoot of the upper whorl should be trained vertically, to replace the damaged one. Any competing shoots should be cut out, or reduced by one third of their length. This establishes apical dominance in the replacement leader.

A pollarded Salix (willow), used as a shade tree in a car parking area.

1. to prevent a tree forming a framework of thick heavy branches. This is especially useful for trees which have a habit of letting branches fall from the tree for no apparent reason (branch shedding), e.g. *Populus* (Poplar)
2. to produce a tree with lots of thin, whippy new growth, *Salix* (willows) often produce young branches which have an attractive bark in the winter
3. to produce a small canopy of branches, which do not cast dense shadows on the ground below.

To develop a pollarded tree, the plant is allowed to grow as a single stem until it reaches a desired height (usually 2m (6ft) minimum). In the winter, all the side branches are removed to leave stubs of growth 5cm (2ins) long.

This severe pruning will lead to a mass of new shoots developing in the spring and summer, and some of these branches may need thinning to prevent weak stems forming due to overcrowding. Any shoots which form on the trunk are cut off as they emerge. This method of pruning is usually carried out every other year, in order to keep the tree in good condition and not drain away too much of its natural vigour, especially during the first five years after establishment.

POLLARDING

Winter
Cut off all the side branches to leave stubs of growth 5cm (2ins) long.

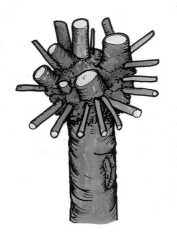

Summer
Thin overcrowded branches to prevent weak stems forming. Any shoots growing on the trunk are cut off as they emerge.

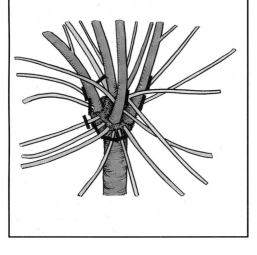

Trees for Pollarding
    Acer cappadocicum 'Aureum',
    A. cappadocicum 'Rubrum',
    A. pennsylvanicum 'Erythrocladum'
    Eucalyptus dalrympleana
    E. pauciflora
    Platanus × *hispanica*
    Populus alba 'Richardii'
    P. × *canadensis* 'Serotina Aurea'
    P. × *candicans* 'Aurora'
    Salix acutifolia 'Blue Streak'
    S. alba 'Britzensis'
    S. a. sericea
    S. a. vitellina
    S. daphnoides 'Aglaia'
    S. matsudana 'Tortuosa'
    S. × *sepulcaris* 'Erythroflexuosa'
    Tilia × *platyphyllos* 'Rubra'

Overcrowded and congested stem growth on a pollarded Salix *(willow).*

ROOT PRUNING

Root pruning (*see* overleaf also) is some-times used as a means of controlling the vigour of trees and to make them produce more flowers. Great care must be taken with grafted specimens (where the roots and top-growth are actually different plants), as cut-ting the roots can actually stimulate the pro-duction of copious amounts of sucker growth from the rootstock.

In the late winter or early spring, dig a trench around the plant you wish to root prune, between 30–60cm (1–2ft) deep with a circumference just wider than the spread of the tree's canopy of branches. Use a pruning saw or loppers to cut through the thick, woody roots; leave the fibrous roots unpruned. For older trees it is advisable to divide the operation into several sections, and prune a third of the root system each year. This is also practised on younger trees growing in exposed conditions, as it reduces the risk of them blowing over.

RENOVATING OLD TREES

Eventually most trees will outgrow their allocated area, or become neglected. A decision then has to be reached as to whether they be should be removed and

ROOT PRUNING

Mark out a trench around the tree just outside the spread of the tree canopy.

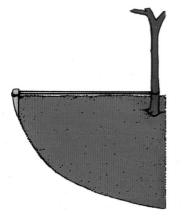

Dig a trench around the tree, between 30–60cm (1–2ft) deep.

Carefully expose all the thick tree roots, and cut out the entire sections of exposed root with a pruning saw or loppers.

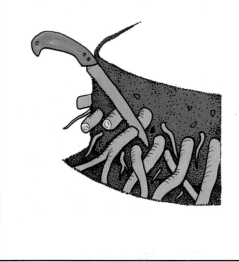

Re-fill the trench with topsoil and firm it well.

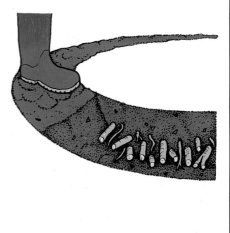

replaced, or an attempt be made to renovate them in order to restore them to full health and vigour. In some cases, a tree may be too old and unsafe to renovate, and replacement is then the only viable alternative. Renovation requires a great deal of patience, care and expertise and with large trees it is always advisable to contact a qualified Arborist (tree surgeon).

Renovation may be carried out at any time of year except in the period from late winter through to late spring for those species which bleed e.g. *Acer* (Maple), *Aesculus* (Horse chestnut), *Betula* (Birch), *Juglans* (Walnut) and *Prunus* (Cherry).

RENOVATION PRUNING

First Year

Cut out any dead, dying, diseased and damaged wood and prune out any crossing and overcrowded branches. Reduce in length any large branches which spoil the balance of the crown.

Second Year

Thin out the new growth to prevent congestion, and create a new framework of branches. Remove any suckers and water shoots.

As with any other form of pruning, the first stage is to remove all dead, dying, diseased and damaged wood. The second stage is to prune out any unwanted growth, such as crossing or congested branches and those which leave the crown of the tree unbalanced.

It is best to carry out extensive renovation over two or three years to allow the tree to recover gradually. If you need to remove any large branches, remove them gradually by cutting them off in sections.

In the year following renovation pruning, the new growth will need to be thinned out

to prevent congestion and leave a well-balanced framework of branches. Any suckers and water shoots should be removed as soon as they appear.

RENOVATING 'HAIRCUT' PRUNED TREES

These are trees which have all of their new growth clipped annually to form a congested cluster of thin, whippy shoots on knobbly branches every year. Such 'haircut' pruning (scalping is a more accurate term) is unsightly and often prevents the production flowers and of course, fruit. This method of pruning also makes the tree more susceptible to fungal infection, due to the large number of cut surfaces.

RENOVATING 'HAIRCUT' PRUNED TREES

Thin out or remove the knotty stumps on the main lateral branches.

Reduce the number of young shoots on remaining stumps to just one or two and cut these back by about one third.

The appearance of these trees can be improved by first thinning out the knotty stumps on the ends of the main branches. Cut out most of the young shoots on the remaining stumps to leave just one or two and prune these back to about one third of their original length. Repeat this procedure in the following three or four seasons to develop a more natural growth habit.

BRANCH REMOVAL

The method of branch removal will obviously vary depending upon the size of the

BRANCH REMOVAL

Using a suitable saw, make an undercut about 30cm (1ft) away from the trunk, cutting up to a quarter of the branch's diameter.

The second cut is on the top of the branch and 5–7.5cm (2–3in) further out from the trunk.

Remove the remaining stub close to the trunk.

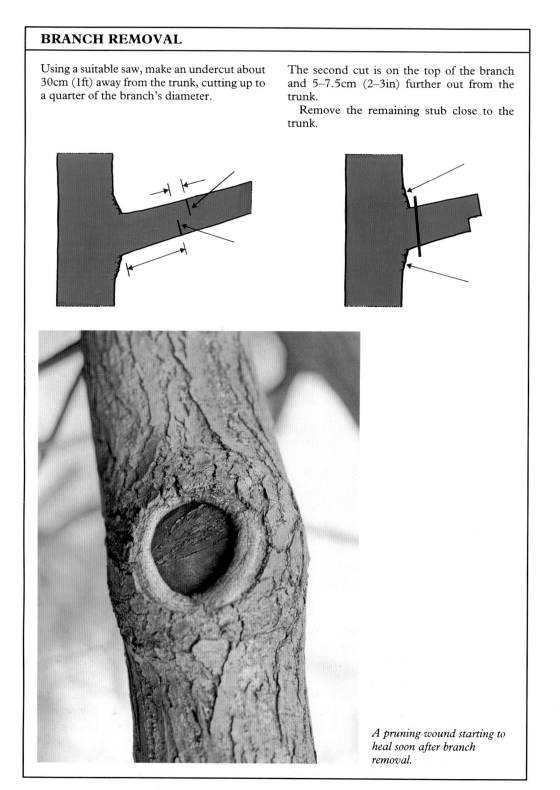

A pruning wound starting to heal soon after branch removal.

On a healthy tree, pruning wounds will eventually heal over completely.

branch and, of course its position above ground level. Small branches can be held with one hand and cut off with a single cut close to the main stem or trunk of the tree. With larger branches, the operation is much more complex as the sheer weight of a large branch obviously creates its own set of problems and difficulties.

It is possible to overcome these problems by adopting a safe pruning procedure which reduces the weight of the branch before the final cuts are made. This can be achieved by making two extra cuts into the branch. The first cut is made on the underside of the branch (called an undercut) at a convenient distance from the trunk. This cut must not go too deep into the wood or the weight of the branch will close the cut and jam the saw.

The second cut is made on the top of the branch and is further out along the branch

*A yew tree (*Taxus baccata*) starting to grow after renovation pruning.*

from the first cut but parallel to it. The distance between these two cuts will depend on the size of the branch but it is normally between 5–7.5cm (2–3in). When the second cut reaches the point where it overlaps the first, the branch will snap along the grain and should fall clear without twisting or tearing. Larger branches can be reduced in sections using this method. The third cut is then made parallel the trunk.

If this procedure is not followed and a large or heavy branch is sawn flush with the trunk, the cut being made from above before some of the weight has been removed, the results can be disastrous. The branch will often tear down into the trunk of the tree causing a large, gaping wound which is a potential site for fungal invasion. If the flush cut is made from the bottom of the branch the weight will cause the saw to jam. It is, therefore, necessary to remove the main part of the branch first.

The main reasons for pruning established trees are:

1. to repair storm damage or other broken branches
2. to remove any dead and dangerous branches
3. to remove crossing branches to avoid rubbing and breakage
4. to crown-thin a tree for one or more of the following reasons:
   (i)   to lessen wind resistance
   (ii) to allow more light and air in through the crown
   (iii) to counteract root damage or structural faults
   (iv) to form and renew a dense crown after heavy lopping
   (v)   to reduce physical and visual 'weight'
   (vi) to reduce leaf volume and therefore leaf nuisance
   (vii) to ensure the safety of people and property
5. to remove lower branches in order to clear pedestrian or vehicle access or to improve traffic sight lines
6. to reduce the overall dimensions of the tree where it has outgrown its allotted space
7. to improve the balance or shape of semi-mature and mature trees.

If you have any doubts about tackling the pruning of larger trees, particularly with the risks involved, always consult a qualified tree surgeon.

TREE SURGEONS

For pruning, renovation, or removal of large trees, it is advisable to consult a qualified tree surgeon. The nearest horticultural college or arboricultural association may be able to supply a list of approved consultants and contractors who comply with required standards of safe working practices and technical competence. Before inviting contractors to tender, decide exactly what work is required, including the disposal of debris (this is often the single most expensive item).

TREE PRESERVATION ORDERS (TPOs)

Under the Town & Country Planning Acts, the Government has delegated powers to local planning authorities, allowing them to make orders which protect trees from unnecessary felling or mutilation. This means that it is an offence to permit, or undertake work without having first gained permission. There have been instances of individuals paying very hefty fines for carrying out work without gaining permission. It is advisable to check the legal position when considering having work carried out on trees. Always assume that your trees are covered by a TPO and contact the local authority's Arboricultural Officer.

CHAPTER 10

Indoor Plants

PRUNING INDOOR PLANTS

Indoor plants require regular pruning to
retain their vigour and promote flowering,
and to improve the growth habit. These
techniques should only be applied when the
plant is well-rooted and actively growing.

As most of the plants grown indoors
have a longer growing season than their
outdoor counterparts, they can look
rather jaded from time to time, and may
need regular pruning on a 'little and often'
basis. Others simply outgrow the available
space, or need cutting back to retain a balanced framework. Whether pruning the
spurs to encourage flowering, cutting back
severely to restrict growth, or just pinching out to encourage bushy growth, some
form of training and shaping is needed by
most plants, even if only to keep the plant
tidy.

As a general rule, the growth of indoor
plants tends to be softer and more tender
than the growth of plants growing outside,
so very sharp tools should always be used. A
sharp knife is ideal for working on the soft-
est stems, with a pair of secateurs being the
best choice for woody stems.

Pruning to Restrict Growth

Under glass, space for shrubs and climbers
is always limited. Although major problems
can be avoided by choosing the most suitable plants for the size of the conservatory
or greenhouse, it may be necessary to
restrict growth to prevent plants blocking
out the light.

*The rapid growth of indoor plants tends to be much
more soft and tender, and may require pruning
more frequently.*

Climbers, particularly those which are
growing in the border soil have to be strict-
ly managed and controlled when they have
filled their allotted space otherwise they
may well overwhelm other plants. Many

climbing plants will grow much more rapid-ly when grown indoors, and this often leads to the plant shedding its leaves, particularly on the bottom third. This bareness at the base of the plant can really only be solved by regular pruning and training.

Training

Annual ornamental climbers or fruiting plants may be tied with soft string to canes placed vertically at regular intervals. Alter-natively, lower a length of strong string or wire from a secure, fixed point in the roof down to the base of the plant. Tie the sup-port loosely around the stem beneath the plant's lowest leaves. The stem can now be loosely twisted around the string as it grows. Never allow the string to become too tight around the stem of the plant.

Plant Supports

Training on supports is essential for climbing plants, as well as being beneficial for a num-ber of non-climbers, such as *Hydrangea*, where stems are brittle or flower heads are heavy. True climbers will use their own means of support, but wall shrubs and some climbers (vines) will require fastening to some artificial support. If ties are used, do not tie plant stems too tightly to the support.

Train new growth before it has become long enough to be untidy and before it becomes too woody and difficult to tie into the support. A few untrained shoots trailing down from the plant can improve its appear-ance, but this should always be planned and not merely the result of neglect.

The basic principles of training and prun-ing under cover are much the same as for outdoors, although it may be necessary to adapt these to accommodate the extended growing period and restricted space.

Some plants flower only on the new sea-son's growth, and on these the old growth may be safely cut back in the spring without

harming the production of next season's flowers. Others flower on older wood, and should only be cut back after flowering.

Timing

The best time for pruning depends on:

1. The plant's flowering season

   Some plants may flower in several flushes. These can be lightly pruned between flushes, while others will flower almost continuously throughout the growing season. These should be pruned immediately after flowering. The time of flowering varies from species to species. Those plants which flower for much of the year under glass will need to be pruned to keep them under control.

2. Whether the plant produces flowers on new or old wood

   Some plants such as *Jasminum polyan-thum*, *Passiflora caerulea*, *Plumbago auricu-lata* and *Solanum* only flower on the cur-rent season's growth, which makes it safe to cut back the old shoots in the spring without harming the formation of the next season's flowers. This should leave lots of room for the new flowering growth.

Few shrubs and ornamental climbers grown under glass flower on old wood, and so should be pruned immediately after flow-ering. However, if you remove the older stems of *Hoya carnosa*, the plant is robbed of most of it's flowering spurs which, year after year, make a big contribution to flower production. Cut back over-vigorous stems in autumn and remove stray shoots when-ever they appear, regardless of the time of year the plant involved is usually pruned.

Some plants flower for much of the year under glass, yet they need to be pruned to control them. In the early spring, cut out

Solanum capsicastrum *(the Christmas cherry) grown for its tomato-like fruits.*

Beleperone guttata *(the shrimp plant) has a tendency to become very straggley as it gets older.* (below)

Varieties of Schefflera *(the umbrella plant) can be pruned at any time of year.*

the previous season's growth on mature *Abutilon* hybrids, and cut back other plants, such as Hibiscus.

THE DESIRED PURPOSE OF PRUNING

Formative Pruning

Certain plants, for example *Coleus*, should be branched and bushy. To make side shoots develop, pinch out the growing point. Many trailing plants get out of hand if not pruned or stopped. *Tradescantia* puts out straggly trailing growth which must be pinched out periodically. With climbing plants, however, the opposite effect is desired, and one or

more strong main shoots should be selected and trained as required. In the spring, the weak side shoots should be cut out cleanly at their junction with the trained stems.

Much of the formative pruning used to improve plant shape and flowering is carried out by 'stopping' or 'pinching'. This usually involves removing the soft growing tips of shoots to encourage the production of new branching shoots.

Routine Pruning

For many plants, no regular pruning is required, but always cut out dead and diseased stems. In order to keep the plant within its allotted area, and keep the competition between plants fairly even, cut back

Beware! When pruned, Poinsettia's exude a white sap which is poisonous.

over-long vigorous shoots. Overcrowded growth should be thinned out by removing any spindly shoots. All growths may be shortened by two thirds every other year, to keep the plants in shape, and prevent the plant becoming bare at the base. Leave a framework of short, spur-like growths as the sites for new growth and flowers.

With variegated plants, cut any green shoots back to their point of origin. These green shoots grow more strongly than their variegated counterparts and will soon swamp them if left to grow unimpeded.

Some flowering plants, such as *Fuchsia*, *Pelargonium* and *Hydrangea* bear their blooms on new growth and these will need to be pruned quite hard at the end of the flowering season. Rampant growing plants should normally have some of their excess stems removed annually. Thin out any tangled stems in early spring (always taking out the older stems). This will result in more air being admitted to the stem, and this will allow better ripening of younger shoots.

Remedial Pruning

This is used for plants which are getting too large and usually consists of pruning back the lateral growths to about 8cm (3in) in the early spring. Also reduce the leading shoots to approximately half of their original length.

Any major operations which involve fairly drastic pruning of main stems and side shoots are best carried out at the start of the active growing season. This is when the plants respond most quickly, and the dormant buds are stimulated into rapid extension growth.

Severe pruning is required only to renovate an overgrown or neglected plant or to remove old, weakened sections of an established specimen.

Temperature

For many plants grown indoors, temperature will have a direct bearing on their growth rate and habit. Plants such as Ivy and *Philodendron scandens* produce growth bearing abnormally small and pale leaves if kept too warm during winter. This growth should be cut back to the first good leaf when spring arrives.

It is important that the remaining stems are not crushed. Cuts made on very thick stems which would tend to 'bleed' if not treated should be dusted with powdered charcoal immediately after pruning.

CITRUS

No regular pruning is required, but all growths may be shortened by two-thirds every other year, to keep the plants in shape and prevent the plant becoming bare at the base. The best time to do this is in the early spring.

FORMATIVE PRUNING

Spring
Pinch out the growing point of the plant when the main stem reaches a height of 30–40cm (12–16in).

Summer
As the new lateral shoots develop, pinch them back to 10–15cm (4–6in), to form a bushy plant.

CLIMBING PLANTS FOR GROWING INDOORS

PRUNE AFTER FLOWERING	PRUNE AS REQUIRED
Allemanda cathcartica 'Hendersonii'	*Agapetes macrantha*
Bougainvillea	*Asarina erubescens*
Clerodendrum thomsoniae	*Cissus*
Distictis buccinatoria	*Cobaea scandens*
Jasminum	*Gynura aurantiaca*
Kennedia rubicunda	*Hoya*
Mandevilla splendens	*Ipomoea horsfalliae*
Pandorea jasminoides	*Monstera deliciosa*
Passiflora, most	
Solanum wendlandii	
Stephanotis floribunda	
Thunbergia	

ROUTINE PRUNING

This plant will often flower almost continuously and routine pruning is carried out throughout the year.

Summer/Autumn/Winter
Remove the dead flowers as they start to fade, but pull off the flowers only or the minute fruits (mini oranges) will be destroyed. Cut out and dead, damaged and diseased shoots.

Spring
Trim back the remaining growths by up to two thirds of their original length, to keep the plant in shape.

HIBISCUS ROSA-SINENSIS – FORMATIVE PRUNING

First Year

Spring
Pinch out the growing point of the plant when the main stem reaches a height of 30cm (1ft).

Summer
As the new lateral shoots develop and become woody, pinch them back to 10cm (4in) to form a bushy plant.

HIBISCUS ROSA-SINENSIS

Prune these plants hard immediately after the flowers have finished. Any growth which is overcrowded should be thinned out by cutting the shoots back to spurs 8cm (3in) long. All thin, spindly shoots should be cut back to their point of origin. The remaining growth can then be reduced to approximately half of its original length. This will encourage plenty of new shoots which will carry the next season's flowers.

HIBISCUS ROSA-SINENSIS – ROUTINE PRUNING

Summer
Remove the dead flowers as they start to fade.

Autumn
Start by cutting out dead, damaged and diseased shoots. Thin out any overcrowded growths, and remove any thin, weak shoots. The remaining growths should be reduced to approximately half of their original length.

Spring
Thin out any weak overcrowded shoots which may have formed as a result of the autumn pruning.

MONSTERA – FORMATIVE PRUNING

Spring
Initially, train the new plant against a moss pole so that the roots can anchor the plant.

Remove any damaged leaves.

MONSTERA

If the plant becomes too tall, remove the growing tip in July, cutting back to a point just above a leaf. The two or three buds immediately below this point will develop and produce new lateral shoots. This plant is usually grown against a moss pole, so that the roots can penetrate the moss to anchor the plant.

STEPHANOTIS

This fast-growing plant is often trained around a wire hoop to try and contain its

MONSTERA – REMEDIAL PRUNING

Summer
When the plant becomes too tall, cut back the main stem and any lateral branches to a point just above a leaf. New lateral shoots will develop from the two or three buds immediately below the point where the cut was made.

Retie the remaining shoots to the support.

MONSTERA – ROUTINE PRUNING

Spring
Thin out any overcrowded growths, and remove any thin, weak shoots. The remaining growths should be tied into position until they become anchored to the support.

Remove any damaged leaves.

STEPHANOTIS –
FORMATIVE PRUNING

Spring
Select and train one or more strong main shoots around the support framework as required. Cut out any weak, side shoots at their junction with the trained stems.

Pinch out the growing point of the plant when the main stem reaches a height of 30–40cm (12–16in).

ROUTINE PRUNING

Spring
Cut out all weak, lateral growths in the early spring, prune back the lateral growths to about 8cm (3in) and reduce the leading shoots to approximately half of their original length.

REMEDIAL PRUNING

Spring
Untwine the stems from the support, remove all the dead, and diseased growth first, cut off all the old growth and leave just two or three new, vigorous shoots.

Rewind the remaining shoots around the support.

straggly, untidy habit. Cut out all weak lateral growths in the early spring. Routine pruning consists of pruning back the lateral growths to about 8cm (3in) in the early spring. At the same time, the leading shoots are reduced to approximately half of their original length.

Remedial pruning for plants which are getting too large involves unravelling all the stems from the support, and cutting off all the old growth, leaving just two or three new vigorous shoots.

SINNINGIA (GLOXINIA)

These plants require the minimum of pruning. Remove the flowers as they fade and

SINNINGIA (GLOXINIA) –
ROUTINE PRUNING

Summer
Cut out the flowers as they fade and start to collapse, taking the flower stalk along with the spent flower.

Remove the dead leaves as they dry off and turn brown after flowering.

Pruning and training can produce plenty of flowers as well as the desired shape of the plant.

start to collapse, taking out the flower stalk along with the spent flower, as this will prevent seed forming and draining the plant of energy. After flowering has finished, allow the plant to gradually dry off, removing the dead leaves as they turn brown.

Glossary

Adventitious bud A bud which arises in an unusual or unplanned place

Alternate (buds/leaves) Leaves which occur at different levels on opposite sides of the stem

Apical bud The uppermost bud in the growing point of a stem (also known as the terminal bud)

Auxins Plant growth substances which occur naturally in the plant

Axil The angle at the point where the leaf or branch joins the main stem of a plant

Axillary bud A bud which occurs in the leaf axil

Backfill The operation of refilling a trench or hole in the ground

Bare-root Plants which are offered for sale with no soil on their roots (usually grown in the field and dug up for sale)

Bark A protective layer of cells on the outer surface of the roots and stems of woody plants

Bark-ringing The practice of removing a ring of bark from the trunk of a tree to help control vigour

Biennial bearing A plant which slips into a habit of producing fruit on a two-year cycle

Bleeding The excessive flow of sap from spring-pruned plants

Blind bud A bud which fails to produce a terminal bud

Branch A shoot growing directly from the main stem of a woody plant

Break A shoot growing from a bud as a result of pruning

Broad-leaved Deciduous or Evergreen plants which have flat, broad leaves

Bud A condensed shoot containing an embryonic shoot or flower

Bud union The point where a cultivar is budded onto a rootstock

Bush A multi-branched plant with a number of branches of similar size

Callus The plant tissue which forms as a protective cover over a cut or wounded surface

Cambium A layer of reproductive cells which are responsible for stem thickening and healing

Climber
A self-supporting plant capable of growing vertically

Collar
The point on the plant where:
  a) the roots begin at the base of the main stem
  b) the swollen area where a branch joins the main stem

Compound leaf A leaf consisting of a number of small segments (leaflets)

Conifer A classification of plants which have naked ovules often borne in cones, and narrow, needle-like foliage

Coppicing The severe pruning of plants to ground level on an annual basis

Cordon A tree trained to produce fruiting spurs from a main stem

Cultivar A plant form which originated in cultivation rather than having been found growing in the wild

Dead-heading The deliberate removal of dead flower-heads or seed-bearing fruits

Deciduous Plants which produce new leaves in the spring and shed them in the autumn

Dieback The death of plant growth downwards from the shoot tip

Dormancy A period of reduced growth through the winter

Epicormic shoots Shoots which develop from dormant adventitious buds on the main stem of a plant (often referred to as 'water shoots')

Espalier A tree trained to produce several horizontal tiers of branches from a vertical main stem

Evergreen Plants which retain their actively growing leaves through the winter

Feathered A young tree with small lateral branches (feathers)

Formative Pruning A pruning method carried out on young plants to establish a desired plant shape and branch structure

Framework The main permanent branch structure of a woody plant

Fruit The seed-bearing vessel on a plant

Graft union The point where a cultivar is grafted onto a rootstock

Grafting A propagation method involving the joining of two or more separate plants together

Half standard A plant of bushy habit growing on a single stem with the lowest branch forming 1–1.5m (3–5ft) above soil level

Lateral A side shoot arising from an axillary bud

Leader The main dominant shoot or stem of the plant (usually the terminal shoot)

Leaf The main lateral organ of a green plant

Leaflet One of the small segments of a compound leaf

Loppers Long-handled, secateur-like pruners used for pruning thicker branches

Maiden A young (one-year-old) budded or grafted tree or bush

Meristem Plant tissue which possesses the capacity to divide and multiply (found in buds, roots and stems)

Mulch A layer of material applied to cover the soil

Opposite Where leaves, buds or stems are arranged in pairs arranged directly opposite one another

Pinching out The removal (usually with finger and thumb) of a plant's growing point of a shoot to encourage the development of lateral shoots

Pollarding The severe pruning of a tree's main branches to the main stem or trunk

Rambler A vigorous trailing plant with a scrambling habit

Renewal pruning A pruning system based on the systematic replacement of lateral fruiting branches

Root The underground support system of a plant

Root ball The combined root system and surrounding soil/compost of a plant

Root pruning The cutting of live plant roots to control the vigour of a plant

Rootstock The root system onto which a cultivar is budded or grafted

Sap The juice or blood of a plant

Scion The propagation material taken from a cultivar or variety to be used for budding or grafting

Shoot A branch stem or twig

Sideshoot A stem arising from a branch stem or twig

Spur A short fruit/flower bearing branch

Standard A tree with a clear stem of at least 1.8m (6ft)

Stem The main shoot of a tree

Stooling The severe pruning of plants to within 10–15cm (4–6in) of ground level on an annual basis

Stone fruits A term usually reserved for fruit-bearing members of the genus *Prunus* e.g. apricot, cherry, damson, plum

Stopping Cutting out the growing point of a shoot to encourage the development of lateral shoots

Sub-lateral A side shoot arising from an axillary bud of a lateral shoot

Sucker A shoot arising from below ground level

Tap root The large main root of a plant

Terminal bud The uppermost bud in the growing point of a stem (also known as the apical bud)

Thinning The removal of branches to improve the quality of those remaining

Tip prune Cutting back the growing point of a shoot to encourage the development of lateral shoots

Tree A woody perennial plant usually consisting of a clear stem or trunk and a framework or head of branches

Trunk The main stem of a mature tree

Union (graft union) The point where a cultivar is grafted onto a rootstock

Variegated Plant parts (usually leaves) marked with a blotched irregular pattern of colours such as gold or silver on a base colour of green

Vegetative growth Non-flowering stem growth

Water shoots Shoots which develop from dormant adventitious buds on the main stem of a plant (often referred to as 'epicormic shoots')

Whip A young one-year-old tree with no lateral branches

Whorl The arrangement of three or more leaves, buds or shoots arising from the same level

Wind-rock The loosening of a plant's roots caused by wind

Wound Any cut or damaged area on a plant

Wound paint A paint or paste applied to cover a cut or damaged area on a plant

Index